*But the LORD has taken you, and brought
you forth out of the iron furnace, out of
Egypt, to be a people of his own
possession.*—Deuteronomy 4:20 RSV

*You shall say to them, "Thus says the
LORD, the God of Israel: Cursed be the man
who does not heed the words of this
covenant which I commanded your fathers
when I brought them out of the land of
Egypt, from the iron furnace, saying,
Listen to my voice, and do all that
I command you. So shall you be my
people, and I will be your God.*
—Jeremiah 11:3-4 RSV

DISARMING the SECULAR GODS

How to Talk So Skeptics Will Listen

Peter C. Moore

Foreword by J. I. Packer

INTERVARSITY PRESS
DOWNERS GROVE, ILLINOIS 60515

InterVarsity Press is the book-publishing division of InterVarsity Christian Fellowship, a student movement active on campus at hundreds of universities, colleges and schools of nursing. For information about local and regional activities, write Public Relations Dept., InterVarsity Christian Fellowship, 6400 Schroeder Rd., P.O. Box 7895, Madison, WI 53707-7895.

Distributed in Canada through InterVarsity Press, 860 Denison St., Unit 3, Markham, Ontario L3R 4H1, Canada.

Cover graphic: TRANSLIGHT

ISBN 0-8308-1270-9

Printed in the United States of America ∞

Library of Congress Cataloging-in-Publication Data
Moore, Peter Childress.
    Disarming the secular gods: how to talk so skeptics will listen/
Peter C. Moore; foreword by J. I. Packer.
      p.   cm.
    Includes bibliographical references.
    ISBN 0-8308-1270-9
    1. Apologetics—20th century. 2. Skepticism—Controversial
literature. I. Title.
    BT1102.M653   1989
    239—dc20   89-36756
                                       CIP

16	15	14	13	12	11	10	9	8	7	6	5	4	3	2
99	98	97	96	95	94	93	92	91	90					

Foreword

When I was a child, I made tunnels. I made them in the yard at home, using a trowel, and on ocean beaches, using a sand spade. First I dug approaches, slanting down to what were to be the tunnels' two mouths; then, with a rotary motion of the trowel or spade, I scooped out my headings till the magic moment came when they met and my tunnel was complete. Success!

When I got older, I found that this is just how professional tunneling is done. Headings started at each end, often miles apart, are extended till they meet in the middle. I suppose that for engineers the technical skill that this involves is mere routine, but to a tunnel lover like me it brings amazement and joy every time, and I expect always will.

When I became a Christian and started sharing my faith, I discovered that apologetics (by which I mean the task of commending Christianity to thinking people as needed truth) is much like tunneling. A way for the Lord must be driven through the naturally hard human heart. Starting from one end, you pile up reasons for receiving Christ's gospel as truth; starting from the other, you try to show that what this gospel and its Christ are offering is the answer to a universal need. When God makes these two headings meet in people's hearts, convincing them both that Jesus Christ is for real and that their only hope is to turn to him, conversion follows. On its horizontal plane the Christian life holds no greater privilege than by thus tunneling to help another person into a living relationship with the incarnate Lord.

Peter Moore is a gifted tunneler of this kind, passionate and skillful in his life purpose of leading the thoughtless to reflection and through reflection to full Christian faith. Honed among teen-agers and undergraduates, audiences that soon switch off from what fails to ring true, Peter's come-think-with-me style has both precision and power for opening shuttered minds to Christian realities. It has been said that if you open your mind wide enough, much rubbish will be poured into it, and that is no doubt true; but the deeper truth is that openness to reality is the basic intellectual virtue, without which, however long you exist, you never quite live. This book is an invitation to live, and the clear way in which it applies the rationality of faith to the wistful willfulness of our time opens the mind to the *wisdom* of Christianity in compelling fashion. Read, mark, learn and inwardly digest!

J. I. Packer

Preface

I was never taught apologetics. By the time I attended theological seminary at the end of the 1950s, theology had turned in on itself. Like many other branches of knowledge it had developed a language of its own and an intellectual elite who disdained controversy with those on the outside, or had forgotten how to do it. While the elite invited others to explore the depths with them, they refused to wade into the shallow waters of ideological dispute with those who rejected theology's most basic premise: God is. In the post-World War 2 years, some, like C. S. Lewis, were writing apologetics and gaining a wide readership. But they were not read by those who taught me theology. Lewis, for instance, was considered a popularizer and, despite his great learning in Medieval languages and literature, he was thought to have oversimplified things from the perspective of the true theologians. The repartee between Lewis and Norman Pittenger which *The Christian Century* printed in 1958 was a case in point.

But I used apologetics. Yale in the 1950s was not exactly a hotbed of orthodox faith. As an undergraduate I continually found myself discussing issues of belief with skeptical classmates, even though I had not announced myself a candidate for the ministry and had no immediate plans to attend seminary. But, as a believer, I was conscious of standing out, and others who were either searching or in various stages of rebellion found my apparent certainty a challenge. Few meals would go by in the Timothy Dwight College dining hall that didn't turn into minidebates about this Christian idea or that. I found it curious that I should have been assigned to this particular residential college, named after the illustrious and pious nineteenth-century grandson of Jonathan Edwards, whose apologetic zeal, as president of Yale, challenged the arguments of the Enlightenment and reversed the tide of skepticism which was sweeping the university.

All that I had gleaned from reading this source or that came in handy. But I was conscious that my resources were limited, and there were few to whom I could turn. In the face of challenge, however, one learns fast, and I was soon encouraged to find that I was not as alone as I had thought. Speakers who came through New Haven encouraged the saints, and visiting InterVarsity staff were supportive. I eventually discovered that I was part of a growing post-World War 2 resurgence of confidence in the intellectual credibility of the biblical faith. Yes, Peter, there are answers, even if your university surroundings are telling you that there are only questions.

I did in the end decide to study theology, but not to go directly to seminary. After graduation and theological studies in England, I returned to plow my energies into student work. Therein lies another tale outside the scope of this book, but suffice it to say that for the next twenty-five years I became a professional apologist for the Christian faith. In the midst of my career as a minister to America's independent secondary schools, one headmaster bestowed on me the title of "apostle to the preppies," a label which I chose to wear with honor. It is out of the experience of those years that the material in this book comes.

There have been various guinea pigs on whom the material in these chapters was tested, and whose comments and criticisms have been invaluable to me in putting it into its final form. Students in schools and colleges from Atlanta to Knoxville to Williamstown, Massachusetts, have had to endure lectures on the modern "isms" which rival Christian faith. It was encouraging to feel that the material contained here was relevant to their concerns, even if its form needed fine tuning. For that process I am particularly indebted to a number of people who read the manuscript and gave me helpful comments. After reading it Michael Green encouraged me with a note: "You must publish it!" Stephen Smith gave me many helpful tips, as did Brian Walsh. Their observations and suggestions carried a great deal of weight because apologetics is their professional field. Ray Anderson was insightful also, as was Jack Rogers. Denyse O'Leary sharpened up both form and content with her painstaking editorial work on an early draft. Martin Gamble also gave me helpful notations. I am especially indebted to Jim Packer, a long-time mentor and friend, for his helpful foreword.

This book was originally entitled *Out of the Iron Furnace: Exit Routes from Today's Secular Faiths.* Lifted from the two obscure biblical texts which are printed just before the title page, the title was an author's dream but a publisher's and bookseller's nightmare. Having discovered the texts, which speak of Israel's exodus in vivid terms as a deliverance from the iron furnace of Egypt, I dreamed for years of weaving a book around the exodus theme. Hence the reader will discover quotes on this theme preceding each chapter, and the footprints of a modern skeptic's exodus lightly sketched here and there in the text. But, with a pragmatism that I could not resist, my wise editor and old friend Jim Hoover suggested the present title. It does the job of conveying the essence of the book with simple clarity. I am very happy with it.

Thinking back on the years it took me to put this in final form, I am enormously grateful to IBM for developing the computer! I am also deeply indebted to my family for their indulgence in cordoning off many hours of what could have been "family time" so that I could work on it, and most especially am I grateful to my wife, Sandra, my most loyal critic, to whom I dedicate this book.

Joseph said to his brothers, "I am about to die; but God will visit you, and bring you up out of this land to the land which he swore to Abraham, to Isaac, and to Jacob." Then Joseph took an oath of the sons of Israel, saying, "God will visit you, and you shall carry up my bones from here." So Joseph died, being a hundred and ten years old; and they embalmed him, and he was put in a coffin in Egypt.   (*GENESIS 50:24-26*)

I Have a Dream
The Apologist's Task

APOLOGETICS *SOUNDS LIKE THE COMMON WORD* APOLOGY, which we all know means to say you are sorry. But its meaning is quite different. According to Webster, apologetics is "that branch of theology devoted to the defense of religious faith addressed primarily to criticism originating from outside the religious faith; especially: such defense of the Christian faith." Apologetics comes from the Greek word *apologeomai,* meaning "to make reply," "to make a legal defense of oneself." An *apologia* is, then, a formal defense or justification of a person or a position. When Cardinal Newman entitled his famous autobiography *Apologia Pro Vita Sua,* he was offering no regrets. He was simply building a case or giving reasons for the path he had chosen.

Is there a difference, though, between what Newman did and what the Christian apologist does? Newman was defending his own personal faith. Specifically he was giving reasons for his abandonment of Anglicanism in favor of Roman Catholicism. It was a highly personal statement. The Christian apologist, however, is not defending his own personal faith. As C. S. Lewis once told a group of Anglican priests and youth leaders in Wales: "Each of us has his individual emphasis: each holds, in addition to the Faith, many opinions which seem to him to be consistent with it and true and important. . . . But we are defending Christianity, not 'my religion.' "[1]

Keeping this in mind, we find that the task of the Christian apologist is threefold. First of all, to defend Christians. This seems an almost impossible task, and for this very reason many give up right here. History books are filled with stories of terrible things done in the name of Christianity by professing Christians. The Crusades, so frequently mentioned by schoolboys and schoolgirls, are only the tip of the iceberg. There is the Inquisition, religious wars, the Salem witch trials, to name a few more. Much of this is sad, but true.

Exaggerations abound, however. I have heard it argued that the blame for the Nazi Holocaust should be laid at the feet of Christians, for it was Christian prejudice against the Jews that created the social climate within which a "Final Solution" such as Hitler's could be hatched. Or, to take another example, in a 1960s article later published in *The Ecology Handbook*, Lynn White, Jr., claimed that the real reason for our ecological crisis was a Judeo-Christian disregard for the earth that was rooted in the Bible's dualism between man and nature, and God's command to "rule" (or, as White claimed, "exploit") his natural environment.[2]

Charges against Christians of one sort or another go back to the earliest days of the church. In the first century Christians were accused of civil disobedience (because they disrupted society), of atheism (because they would not participate in official emperor worship), of cannibalism (because they ate of the "body and blood" of Christ), of sexual immorality (because they loved each other and were not afraid of saying so), and of philosophical absurdity (because they spoke of God becoming a human being). Of these, the charge of civil disobedience became the most serious.

When the Roman Empire called for a loyalty oath, "Caesar is Lord," the Christians said, "No! Jesus is Lord." The confession "Jesus is

Lord" appears to have been the first and most basic of all the Christian creeds, going back as early as A.D. 55, where, in Paul's letter to the Corinthians, it seems already to have been in common usage.[3] It is generally recognized that the book of Acts was written, in part, to answer charges that the Christians were dangerous people. When its author, Luke, wrote that the Christians "had favor with all the people," he had one ear cocked to the criticisms that were so common in his day, and to become even more common in the days to come.[4]

The point of defending Christians is not, of course, to whitewash reprehensible behavior. There is a place for Christians to confess, in shame, things which have been done in the name of Christ. But the specific charges leveled against Christians are often unfounded and contrived, and even in cases where the charges are accurate, it is usually because believers have not followed the teachings of Christ.

Some of the earliest Christian apologists were particularly concerned to answer charges that could lead to serious misunderstanding. Justin Martyr, writing in A.D. 153, addressed his words to the Emperor Antoninus Pius, saying that if he was concerned about piety and wisdom he had nothing to fear from Christians. "We are your best allies in securing good order." And other second-century apologists pointed to the integrity of the Christian community's sexual morality when compared to the general culture.[5]

Martyrdom did much to prove the integrity of Christian character, enabling later apologists to turn their attention to combating rival world views like Gnosticism, which was a combination of Greek and Oriental thought fashionable in the second century. These apologists made much of the claim in the Gospel of John that Jesus is the divine Logos, arguing that this meant that Jesus was the embodiment of the basic principle of harmony and order in the universe—something for which the Greeks were always searching.

History Is Not Bunk
In apologetics a second and far more basic aim than defending Chris-

tians is that of defending Christian claims. Christianity is the only nonethnic world religion to make spiritual truth depend on historical events. It would matter little to the teachings of Buddhism, Islam or Confucianism if the Buddha, Muhammad or Confucius had never lived. But with Christianity the events of Christ's life, death and resurrection are essential. As St. Paul says, if Christ has not been raised from the dead as a historical fact, our faith crumbles to the ground.[6]

It is often quite rightly pointed out that, in distinction to other religions, the Bible speaks of a God who acts in history. As an idea this claim has no force until specific historical events are cited as having been done by God. Herein lies both Christianity's strength and its vulnerability. For as soon as specific historical events are mentioned, the historical skeptics go to work, seeking alternate causes for the events mentioned. More influenced than they should be by the eighteenth-century essayist G. E. Lessing's famous statement that it can never be permissible to base a universal religious truth on the occurrence of a particular event,[7] even many theologians seek to avoid what has been called the "scandal of particularity." But as J. V. Langmead Casserley writes, "the mere idea of an active God who does something is quite as static as the mere idea of a static God who does nothing."[8]

Biblical religion argues in the main from the particular to the general, rather than vice versa. And this needs defending, because not only are the events ascribed to God hard for the modern mind to believe, but also people will tend to think today that anything that happened two thousand years ago is irrelevant. To be sure, no one would argue that the Magna Charta is irrelevant today or the discovery of chloroform—or for that matter, the invention of the wheel. But when Henry Ford made the offhand comment "history is bunk," he betrayed one of the underlying prejudices of the twentieth century.

Therefore, the apologist needs to make a case not only for the specific events of the Incarnation, the miracles of Jesus, the resurrection, the sending of the Spirit and life beyond the grave, but for the entire world view that insists that God broke into the created order at a point in history to save a lost humanity. For in the end the clash between Christianity and other ways of understanding reality stems from differences in world views.

As far as views of history are concerned, there are essentially three options. Either history is (1) a patternless chain of events, (2) a cyclical repetition of events according to some overarching pattern, or (3) a line with a beginning, points along the way and an end. Outside the biblical tradition one finds exponents of the first two. But to the eyes of anyone trained in Judeo-Christian thought, these in effect say, "History is meaningless." That is, both view the details of this or that event as unimportant. What matters is only the pattern in the one case, or the lack of it in the other.

The Bible, however, has a very different conception. God is not just the Lord of creation, the one who starts everything going in accordance with a grand plan. He is also the Lord of history. History is "his story," and in some unfathomable combination of divine sovereignty and human will, God is the master chess player moving his chessmen forward and back in anticipation of the final moment when all that opposes him will be checkmated and his reign will be universally recognized.

The third aim of the Christian apologist is to expose non-Christian assumptions. Often people hold views of which they are quite unaware until someone articulates them for them. We are brought to see ourselves often through the words of others. This happens ever more frequently these days because our training teaches us to think existentially rather than systematically. Thus, instead of seeing logical connections from one idea to another and pursuing a path of thought to its natural conclusion so as to gain a grasp of the whole, we are taught that it is perfectly all right to hold mutually exclusive ideas as true at the same time as long as they somehow fit with our experience.

Therefore, we can be personally opposed to abortion, but unwilling to impose our views on anyone else. We can believe in free speech, but protest bringing to our college campus a speaker whose political views we consider extreme. We can be passionately committed to peace, yet justify violence by the opponents of the regime in South Africa in the name of revolution and a "just war."[9] We can believe that everything originated by chance, and yet hold passionately to the idea that the survival of the human race is a moral absolute.

Part of the apologist's task, then, is to point to differences. It is necessary to show that there is a difference between believing that the universe is created and that the universe has always been. There is a difference between believing that human beings are "fallen" from an original goodness and in need of restoration and believing that as a race we are progressively getting better and better. There is a difference between thinking that there exists a revealed purpose for human life that conforms to God's will and believing that people create their own meaning. Despite the efforts of some to say that all religions teach the same thing, we must reply that it is simply not the same thing to say that people are lost and need a savior as to say that people can, with time, effort and moral resolve, save themselves. To claim that it is possible to know God personally with certainty is not the same as to say that such a claim is sheer nonsense and presumption.

The Point of It All

But, it may be objected, why bother? What is the point of all this verbal warfare? Can't we just live and let live? You have your ideas; I have mine. Let's call it a truce. All this proving of one person right and another wrong has been the cause of endless strife and division. Should we not follow Polonius's advice to Laertes: "To thine own self be true; And it must follow, as the night the day, Thou canst not then be false to any man"?[10]

Setting aside the strange contemporaneity of Shakespeare's wit and wisdom, if we take this line of argument we miss the point. Apologetics, remember, aims not to defend "my religion" over against yours, but to give a reasoned defense of the Christian faith and answer the many charges that have been leveled against it.

It is true that some will never be persuaded by reason. Their minds are closed. "Prejudices are rarely overcome by argument; not being founded in reason they cannot be destroyed by logic."[11] Still, we must not lightly give up the difficult task of pressing for clarity and truth, because ideas influence actions. And unless we are content to approach major issues of life today, like genetic engineering, surrogate parenthood, abortion clinics, affirmative action, pollution control, human rights and a host of other knotty problems, without a point of view, we must enter the debate. Otherwise John Lennon and Paul McCartney's description of the dilemma of their age will fit ours as well:

> He's a real nowhere man
> Sitting in his nowhere land
> Making all his nowhere plans for nobody.
>
> Doesn't have a point of view,
> Knows not where he's going to—
> Isn't he a bit like me and you?

Although we cannot abandon the quest for truth, we enter the debate aware that many will not be reached by any sort of reasoned approach. In a subtle way truth is their enemy. Writing about alienated youth in American society, Yale psychology professor Kenneth Keniston says that one of the marks of alienation is that a person cannot tolerate a true view of things. The alienated feel doubly deprived because they are cut off not only from the "illusions" which other people have, but also from the benefits those "illusions" bring to those who have them: a sense of security, a purpose to life, and a feeling of communion. The alienated, he says, are not rejoicing in the knowledge that God is dead. "Rather they experience anger and rage at their own loss, and then look with contempt on those who still believe in His existence."[12]

Because of the emotion that lies beneath some people's skepticism, therefore, it is important for the apologist to bend over backward to understand and to listen. Nothing is gained by pressing for victory in debate. A man of no mean apologetic gifts himself, the Scottish novelist and poet George Macdonald said:

> When a man argues for victory and not for truth, he is sure of just one ally, that is the devil. Not the defeat of the intellect, but the acceptance of the heart is the only true object in fighting with the sword of the Spirit.[13]

While the apologist must listen, he does not apologize for wanting to win others over to Christ. Ever since the Holy Spirit came upon the one hundred twenty or so disciples on Pentecost, the Christian movement has been unashamedly committed to mission—that is, to the spread of the gospel and the winning of individuals to faith. Without this vision it is doubtful that the fledgling church would ever have spread much beyond the walls of Jerusalem.

Hidden Persuaders

Sadly, much that has gone by the name of evangelism has been manipulative, anti-intellectual and culture-bound. Hence people react as much to the word *evangelism* as to the substance. That is why apologetics is crucial. It clears the ground, answers questions, builds bridges and enables the gospel invitation to be offered to people at the level of both heart and mind.

As a society we are increasingly aware of the seductive approaches which are used to sell products, politicians and even religious cults to the unsuspecting public. Vance Packard's book *The Hidden Persuaders* came and went in the 1960s, but was perhaps most sorely needed in the 1970s when the cult phenomenon burst upon us and led so many naive young people into intellectual captivity and tragically, as in the case of Jim Jones's followers, to death. For the same principles Packard wrote about in the consumer realm are applicable to the religious realm. Quoting the writer Joseph Seldin, Packard wrote:

Manipulation of children's minds in the fields of religion or politics would touch off a parental storm of protest and a rash of Congressional investigations. But in the world of commerce children are fair game and legitimate prey.[14]

Like high-pressure, emotional evangelists, the cult leaders studiously avoided grappling with the minds of those they were seeking to persuade. Marathon teaching sessions, guilt-inducing exhortations, "love-bombing" (surrounding potential recruits with caring people speaking affirming words), mantra chanting and glossolalia were all part of a strategy to bypass minds in an effort to transfix hearts. Once persuaded, some were so lost to even the idea of an open mind that parents began kidnaping their own children in order to deprogram them and win them back to sanity or rationality.

While orthodox Christians watched a mushrooming cult phenomenon with growing apprehension, society as a whole was confused. Are not all convinced believers equally dangerous, they thought? Having neglected to provide their children with a religious foundation, secularized parents panicked at the thought of others winning their children's allegiance to viewpoints far removed from their own. A few even thought drugs would be preferable.

Culture-bound evangelism, then, and the cult phenomenon became lumped together. Both were considered to be manipulative. People could not recognize that many forms of evangelism acknowledge the legitimacy of apologetics. What good is the evangelist's appeal to the heart and conscience if the mind is overlooked? In fact, one sign of the difference between the cults and authentic evangelism is the validity the latter gives to the basic questions people ask.

Evangelism has become synonymous with fundamentalism, which in turn has become a household word synonymous with extremism. Fundamentalism is just as easily applied to fanatics like the Ayatollah Khomeini as to the disgraced Jim and Tammy Faye Bakker. As commonly used today, the word *fundamentalist* has almost completely lost the original designation it had of a conservative Christian believer. Instead it is used today as a term by which one distances oneself from anyone whose religious convictions appear to be inflexible, strong, militant or based on divine revelation.

A Penultimate Thought

There is a further reason for apologetics. The mind is one of the vehicles through which we worship God. Worship today is often thought of as either an action or an experience. But worship is to give ultimate worth to somebody or something. It is "worthship." We do not worship first of all with the mouth, singing hymns, or with the knees, crouching for prayer, or with the ear, listening to a sermon. Worship is not even primarily an experience of the heart—feelings of closeness to God. It is an exercise of the mind. Worship is the mind's humble acquiescence to the fact of God. It is the recognition that God is the fountain of all and the goal of all. We worship when we recognize that we have no significance apart from our relation to God, and no health or happiness until by surrendering the illusion of being the center of the universe, we joyfully celebrate him as that center.

Apologetics becomes therefore a handmaiden to worship. It enables us to worship God with our minds as he commanded: "You shall love the Lord your God with all your heart, and with all your soul, and with all your mind."[15] We recognize that this is extremely difficult when the intellectual climate of the day has "no use for the God hypothesis."[16] We must be prepared to swim upstream intellectually. For while intelligent people most certainly still believe in the truth of Christianity, they do so at the expense of widespread intellectual approval. In a speech entitled "The End of Christendom," Malcolm Muggeridge, the British journalist and former editor of *Punch,* contrasted the fall of Rome at the hands of barbarians with the fall of Christendom at the hands of forces from within:

Our barbarians are home products, indoctrinated at the public expense, urged on by the media, systematically stage by stage, dismantling Christendom, depreciating and deprecating all its values. The whole social structure is now tumbling down, dethroning its God, undermining all its certainties. All this, wonderfully enough, is being done in the name of the health, wealth, and happiness of all mankind. That is the basic scene that seems to me will strike a future Gibbon as being characteristic of the decline and fall of Christendom.[17]

It is, then, out of a desire to counterbalance the secular and skeptical spirit of the age that the apologist seeks to show the ultimate worth of a God-centered view of the world.

Clearing the Fog

And, finally, apologetics aims, in the words of St. Paul, to "equip the saints for ministry." Every Christian is called to ministry. Some are called to the professional, or ordained, ministry, but the vast majority are called to minister wherever God places them and to whomever God sends across their paths. To the question "Who is my neighbor?" Jesus answered for all time: Your neighbor is any person who is needy and within your sphere of influence.

As "saints," or called-out ones, therefore, we must be ready, as the apostle Peter wrote, "at any time to give a quiet and reverent answer to any man who wants a reason for the hope that you have within you."[18] But the ability to answer others' questions presupposes a knowledge of our own ground first. It also presupposes an ability to build bridges from the ground on which we stand to the ground on which the other stands. Equipment for ministry in a secular age like ours requires knowing how to do this. But the contemporary Christian, even the educated Christian, is often ill-equipped for the all-important bridge-building task. As British apologist Harry Blamires pointed out in his book *The Christian Mind*, in the modern church there is a widespread loss of understanding of the crucial components which make up a Christian world view.[19]

Christians must re-Christianize their own thinking. It is a challenging task because, as Christians, we have become accustomed to overlooking those elements in historic Christianity which are particularly offensive to contemporary thought. We may have concluded with the best of intentions that certain aspects of the faith are personally repulsive like hell, or obscure like angels, or confusing like predestination. But re-Christianizing our thinking involves submitting our minds once again to the tutelage of the Spirit through the Word of God and learning to listen to the wisdom of greater minds than our own. What people like Lewis and Blamires insist we must not do is to consider ourselves free to alter the faith whenever it looks perplexing or repellent. Such a "liberal" Christianity is completely stagnant. "Progress is made only into a resisting material."[20] By this Lewis meant that efforts to temper the hard aspects of biblical doctrine actually reduce the probability of anything new happening with regard to a person's faith. It was rather like science, he argued, where an "awkward" element in one's schema often is the occasion which leads to the next discovery.[21]

But the argument of this book is based on the conviction that there is as much misunderstanding even among Christians of viewpoints held by non-Christians as exist in the so-called secular world about Christianity itself. Many of these viewpoints are not full-blown world views, but are rather mental orientations upheld by the assumptions of non-Christian thought. The key is to try to get a hold of where the other person is coming from. It is just as easy for believers to stereotype the thinking of non-Christians as it is for them to stereotype our own. Thus we need to listen not just to the conclusions which other people reach and which they may toss out with great assurance, but more important we need to listen to the premises which have led to those conclusions. To do that we need to come to grips with those thought systems which appeal to the modern mind.

Apologetics, then, is vital for six reasons: First, because Christianity, in distinction from other religious systems, makes truth claims rooted in historical events. Such events not only bear critical investigation, but must be defensible by the ordinary Christian. Second, apologetics is a part of the missionary mandate of a church which is by nature inherently evangelistic. Third, believers must attempt to clear away misconceptions of their views and repudiate guilt by association with cultic expressions of the faith. Fourth, by answering the questions of seekers and skeptics, believers take seriously the total person. Fifth, apologetics calls believers and would-be believers to worship God by enabling their minds to rest in the truthfulness of what their hearts tell them. Finally, apologetics is part of the necessary equipment of lay people for ministry in a world where people, confronted with perplexing questions, need answers.

Mind Games?

When the church father Tertullian asked the now famous question "What has Athens to do with Jerusalem?" he pinpointed one of the most difficult problems for the apologist and one which has divided Christian apologists into two camps. The problem is this: If faith is a function of the emotive, intuitive part of us more than of the intellectual, rational part, is not the whole of apologetics an exercise in futility?

Blaise Pascal, the eighteenth-century scientist and lay theologian, once said, "Le Dieu defini est le Dieu fini!" Define God and you've lost him! The more you attempt to describe, delineate and justify theology, the more you abandon real faith. In reaction to the religious rationalism of his day, Pascal argued that Christianity was primarily an experiential religion. Writing out of a deeply emotional encounter with the gospel, he had good reason to be suspicious of the end result of much of what passed for theology. Like Kierkegaard a century later, Pascal was a prophet of the heart, a voice crying in the wilderness of an arid, intellectualized faith.

One of the modern critics of the Western world's fascination with the powers of reason is Adam Smith, whose book *Powers of Mind* indicts the West for its neglect of the right brain. The left side, the rational side, controls our capacity to count, reason, plan and calculate. He argues that the left brain has taken us about as far as it can go. What we need is a rediscovery of the intuitive, nonverbal, artistic right hemisphere.[22]

Who is to blame for this rationalizing trend in Western thought? The secularists? Not according to sociologist Max Weber, whose work on capitalism laid the blame at the feet of Protestantism. He claimed that it was people like Luther, Calvin and Zwingli who, by destroying the superstitious, magical practices and mythical folklore of Medieval Christian theology, actually substituted a rationalistic faith in its place. Instead of the authority of the Mass, or the saints, or relics, or priests, all authority was derived from the authority of the Word.

One can see how this may have happened, although it is doubtful that Weber understood the nature of Reformation faith. Faith to the Reformers was not just assent to correct doctrine, it was the entrusting of oneself to the grace and mercy of God in Jesus Christ. But Weber may have been correct to link later Protestant scholasticism with the secularization of the modern mind. The Reformation's criticism of all gods except one doubtless created the conditions within which that one God would also be criticized. Also the whole desacralization of nature, fostered by the Renaissance, stimulated an interest in the study of things which called Christianity into question. As Anthony Campolo puts it: "Protestant theology stimulated the scientific discoveries which facilitated religious doubt."[23]

In response to these charges, it has to be argued that the gospel of Christ, which was considered so much folly by the first-century Greeks,[24] may always appear incredible to the skeptical mind. We render the gospel no service, however, if we abandon rationality and flee to a mystical or highly emotional faith. Medieval theology, which had its own serious weaknesses, as the Reformation pointed out, at the very least showed that scholasticism and mysticism were both parts of a fully catholic expression of the faith. Christianity does go beyond the rational, but it does not bypass it. What we in fact need, being people of both left and right brains, is a balance of doctrine and experience, fact and feeling, knowledge and love, debate with the world and service to the world. In short, what we need is a balance of head and heart. Movements that are all heart usually founder on the rocks of skepticism. Those that are all head will tend to get buried in the sands of experience.

Kenneth L. Pike, professor of linguistics at the University of Michigan in the 1950s and 1960s, tells how with considerable frustration he gave up trying to persuade his colleagues on the faculty of the truth of Christianity through argument alone. Unless they were prepared to admit the existence of a personal God and the validity of the Scriptures, he found he made little progress. But he discovered that the witness of a Christian life, together with the kindness, gentleness and thoughtfulness for others that accompany it, can speak a language that even skeptics are not able to slough off. Despite this, he refused to abandon apologetics. "Faith cannot operate . . . without some component of intellectual appreciation of the truth of the historical events." Appropriately, he entitled his book on the integration of scholarship and devotion *With Heart and Mind*.[25]

The Via Media

As an Anglican, or Episcopalian, I am grateful for my church's attempt at balance. Historically, Anglicanism has seen itself as the midpoint between, on the one hand, the radical views of the Puritans, who wanted to strip the church both of the theological substance of Catholicism and also of its form, and, on the other, the sacramentalism of the Roman Catholic Church. While keeping Scripture as its supreme authority, Anglicanism honors reason and tradition as important vehicles through which that authority is grasped. It celebrates the breakthroughs of the Reformation, such as justification by faith alone, but retains the Catholic sense of mystery and the crucial role of the sacraments in deepening that faith.

Unfortunately, the balance has not always been kept. Weak in its theology of the Word and excessive in its reliance on externals, Anglicanism at the popular level, especially in North America, often degenerates to a religion of good taste. Preaching is notoriously untheological, and the laity are abysmally ignorant of the essentials of the Bible. As Richard Holloway puts it in *The Anglican Tradition:*

> Anglicanism [is] decorously ceremonial, often a bit childish in its dependence upon secondary matters, and very slack in its grip upon the really essential core of the Christian Faith, what C. S. Lewis called "mere Christianity," that irreducible minimum of theology and behavior without which you are not really a Christian at all.[26]

Something almost totally absent from North American Anglicanism, but not from its British counterpart, is the presence of a tradition of sound apologists, whose speaking and especially writing have challenged people to grapple with this "essential core" of the faith as it interacts with the secular world. Names from Britain are almost legion: J. B. Phillips, C. S. Lewis, Alan Richardson, John Stott, Michael Green, J. I. Packer, David Watson and many others. But one searches in vain for their peers on this side of the Atlantic.

But Is It Biblical?

Apologetics has its critics at the other end of the ecclesiastical spectrum. Occasionally one hears a query about the legitimacy of apologetics from those who insist that it is not biblical. All we need to reach the secular world is to preach the Word, so it is claimed. Those who will not hear have no excuse. But for all its directness this kind of thinking fails to appreciate the variety of approaches to sharing the good news which is found within the Bible itself.

Paul's approach in Corinth was, to be sure, a very direct approach. To reach this city, awash with moral filth and legendary in the ancient world for corruption and vice,[27] Paul chose a direct approach. But in Athens, where the residents were used to debating and discussing different philosophies, he used a different approach. In Acts 17 we see him finding common ground with his listeners, calling them very religious (v. 22). Gently, he exposes the inadequacy of their present assumptions (v. 23), and then he begins to build with the axiom that God exists (v. 24). Finding links to their philosophers and poets (v. 28), he asserts that God is personally knowable. He then moves to the inevitability of judgment (v. 30) and buttresses his claim concerning the divinity of Jesus with the resurrection (v. 31). Here we see Paul's combination of apologetics with evangelism.

The rationale for this approach is given in Paul's first chapter of Romans. There he claims that although people know that God is and have abundant witness to his existence and moral character in nature, they suppress this knowledge and adopt futile alternatives (vv. 18, 25). The result of this suppression is the emergence of lifestyles of raw self-centeredness. However, pagans are not totally incapable of understanding their plight. In fact, Paul argues that one side of their natures is still capable of agreeing with the truth (v. 32). It is an appeal to this side—the side that still agrees with God and questions his displacement by those who refuse to acknowledge him—that apologetics is addressed.

The Family Quarrel

Even among those who believe in apologetics some significant differences of approach have arisen. We can identify three:

The common ground approach. Some seek to make contact with the secular mind by building bridges to God from people's experiences of transcendence. Taking human experience as their starting point, they build from there. Neo-orthodox theologians, like Emil Brunner, drew upon the twentieth-century experience of angst or lostness, especially as interpreted by the existentialist philosophers like Camus. Neo-liberal theologians, like Harvey Cox and John A. T. Robinson,[28] built on the new post-war mood of optimism and celebration. Neo-conservative theologians, like Peter Berger, take our innate human hunger for order, our indomitable propensity to play, our persistent longing to hope, and our sense of both the just and the comic dimensions to life as "signals of transcendence" which carry us beyond the mere relativity of human experience.[29] I have avoided this approach in this book. It seems to me at best to keep alive in a secular age what Peter Berger calls the "rumor of God." But it is a very long way from that to the certainty of Christian faith.

The evidentialist approach. This approach assumes that people's minds are not so captive to falsehood that they are unable to appreciate a reasoned statement of the truth. While evidentialists acknowledge what has been called the "noetic effects of sin"—that is, that sin not only bends our wills but also distorts our minds so that by ourselves we are incapable of thinking correctly about God—they believe that when people's minds are quickened by the Holy Spirit, they respond to a good argument when they see one.

They are not saying that people already have the basic ideas of God in their subconscious or conscious minds and only need someone to give them a logical foundation for faith. This is the claim of natural theology, which assumes that through nature alone people can arrive at the truth about God. What natural theologians in fact usually arrive at, however, is a hodgepodge of vague concepts about a Supreme Being and the necessity for morals, all based on a rationalistic foundation. This was what the seventeenth-century deists believed and, as Bernard Ramm points out, it was refuted in its day by the arguments of the famous Bishop Joseph Butler, who cleverly wielded reason's club against the rationalists.

In his defense of the idea that nature and Scripture have far more in common with each other than is usually supposed, Butler justified the "possible" truthfulness of many Christian ideas, even though by his insistence that everything must be tested by reason alone, he fell far short of a fully biblical world view. Contrary to Butler the Bible sees reason as dependent on revelation and not vice versa. Biblically it is not "I think, therefore God is"; but rather "God is, therefore I think."[30]

Evidentialists, then, while relying on the Spirit to confirm truth, seek to spell out the compatibility of reason and faith by appealing to the innate logic of Christianity. Augustine, while not strictly an evidentialist, thought that reason and faith needed each other. He found, for instance, that the miracles of Jesus were sound evidences of his authority, as were the many Old Testament prophecies he fulfilled. The nineteenth century abounded with books on Christian evidences, and in the twentieth century names like F. F. Bruce, B. B. Warfield, John Stott, Michael Green, John Gerstner, R. C. Sproul, Clark Pinnock and Josh McDowell would be associated with this school of apologetics.

The presuppositional approach. Parting company with those who build bridges from human experience, on the one hand, and with evidentialists, on the other, are writers who insist that until nonbelievers have come to question the presuppositions on which their conclusions are based, a Christian cannot make any progress with them. Early Christian thinkers like Augustine and Anselm of the fourth and fifth centuries certainly laid the foundation for presuppositionalism by insisting that faith must precede understanding. Today the leading exponent of this approach is Cornelius Van Til, but Abraham Kuyper, and more modern advocates like Rousas Rushdoony, E. J. Carnell for most of his life, Carl F. H. Henry, Francis Schaeffer and Os Guinness are all in varying degrees presuppositionalists.

At its heart, presuppositionalism insists that non-Christians must first come to see the inadequacy of their own systems of belief and then be willing to restructure their thought around the fact of God. God, presuppositionalists assert, is self-attesting. So it is impossible to argue one's way to God, one can only argue one's way from God.[31]

Finding One's Way through the Desert

How, then, should we proceed in our search for a way out of the dilemma of unbelief? Having maps and charts is helpful. But without a compass they can be confusing and misleading. In this case the traveler often has to rely on hunches, falling back on a basic sense of direction.

Following their exodus from Egypt, the Hebrews had to rely on many different methods to get through the Sinai Peninsula. Scouting parties were sent ahead to gather information. Moses' authoritative leadership was crucial. But beyond this they were given two lights to guide them—a bright cloud by day and a pillar of fire by night.

In the journey which you as the reader will take in the forthcoming chapters, you will discover that I have chosen to rely on a variety of methods of guiding people out of the iron furnace of modern skepticism. Each of the following chapters begins with one of the fashionable mindsets of the modern age. I cannot call each of them "world views," comprehensive systems which address the fundamental questions of life. Several unquestionably are world views in this sense: monism, humanism, agnosticism. Others are reactive stances, sets of axioms by which people shield themselves from the bright light of truth: relativism and pragmatism. Still others are cultural trends or mind games by which travelers convince themselves that, after all, it is really better in the desert, and a trip back to Egypt now and then wouldn't be a bad idea: hedonism and narcissism.

My approach, then, has been unashamedly eclectic. I attempt to build bridges by going as far as I can with the criticisms people have of Christianity as they understand it. I see no point in denying the obvious. In my dialog with them my point is to say, "You may be right in what you say is wrong, but are you right in what you say is right?" In this sense I start with people's experience.

I am a presuppositionalist insofar as I ask travelers to question the basis on which they are making their decisions and the framework within which they are judging things to be true or false. I also believe that only God can convince us of himself, and that certainty is only discoverable once we become open to being known by God.

But I am also an evidentialist because I believe that to anyone with a glimmer of faith (and few of us are pure believers or pure skeptics) the claims of Christ and his apostles make eminent sense. In fact, the chapters of this book have been arranged so that these claims may be systematically unfolded.

Monists search for absolute unity. To this quest the Bible speaks of an infinite God, both supreme over nature and desirous of personally revealing himself through nature. To the humanist's great hope in human capacities, the Bible speaks of our being created in the image of God. To the relativist's aversion to black-and-white thinking, the Bible presents us with a Jesus who claims to be the light of the world. To the narcissist's quest for self-esteem, the Bible shows us the paradox of finding ourselves through losing ourselves. To the agnostic's certainty that truth cannot be known, the Bible answers with a miracle that cannot be ignored. To the pragmatist's insistence that truth must "work" to be true, the Bible shows how the risk of faith leads to life with a capital *L*. In the chapter on hedonism I seek to show how the search for pleasure and success fails to come to grips with the inevitability of a final judgment.

My final chapter attempts to demonstrate the grounds for what must inevitably appear to outsiders as the annoying certainty of biblical believers. In case you do not make it to this chapter, let me say at the outset that I believe that because God is personal, the only certainty anyone can have about him is the certainty which God gives. In our finitude we are simply not able, by a series of logical arguments, to arrive at certainty about God. Rather it is God who, by the unveiling of his presence, communicates himself to us. In ways that neither bypass our rationality nor place undue importance upon it, God searches for us and finds us. And it is in that experience of being found that we discover God to be knowable.

The route which this book attempts to take, then, is guided by a path the Bible itself seems to take: from God, to creation, to incarnation, to the cross, to the resurrection, to life in the Spirit and ultimately to final judgment. The traveler will find that these, taken not in isolation but together, point the way from the iron furnace of Egypt, through the heat of the Sinai wilderness, to what St. Paul calls the "glorious freedom of the children of God." By themselves they do not bring certainty. As with Israel, only the pillar of fire by night and the cloud by day, reminders of God's own personal presence, guaranteed a suprarational confidence that Yahweh was in their midst, walking with them step by step. This book attempts to give a rationale for the journey and to tell of some signposts along the way. If as you read these words you can also catch a glimpse of the fire and the cloud, then Joseph's dream of a way out of the iron furnace will become yours.

Now Moses was keeping the flock of his father-in-law, Jethro, the priest of Midian; and he led his flock to the west side of the wilderness, and came to Horeb, the mountain of God. And the angel of the LORD appeared to him in a flame of fire out of the midst of a bush; and he looked, and lo, the bush was burning, yet it was not consumed. And Moses said, "I will turn aside and see this great sight, why the bush is not burnt." When the LORD saw that he turned aside to see, God called to him out of the bush, "Moses, Moses!" And he said, "Here am I." Then he said, "Do not come near; put off your shoes from your feet, for the place on which you are standing is holy ground." And he said, "I am the God of your father, the God of Abraham, the God of Isaac, and the God of Jacob." And Moses hid his face, for he was afraid to look at God.

Then the LORD said, "I have seen the affliction of my people who are in Egypt, and have heard their cry because of their taskmasters; I know their sufferings, and I have come down to deliver them out of the hand of the Egyptians, and to bring them up out of that land to a good and broad land, a land flowing with milk and honey." *(EXODUS 3:1-8)*

Barefoot in the Sand
The New Ager's Perception

THE INABILITY OF MUCH OF THE CHURCH TO COPE WITH
the impact of New Age thinking that is bombarding late twentieth-
century Western culture is vividly illustrated by a woman who told me
of the following conversation she had had with her sixteen-year-old
son. He had called from an expensive and prestigious New England
secondary boarding school situated in the rolling Connecticut coun-
tryside. His school maintained a beautiful chapel (rarely used),
funded a chaplain (rarely listened to) and looked back on a great
tradition of moralistic Christianity (no longer taken seriously by administration or faculty). From a pay phone in the dorm the boy
opened with the following question:

"Hi, Mom. How do you get unconfirmed?"

The mother did what any parent would do under the circumstances.
She asked for clarification. "Why, Johnny, what do you mean?"

"How do you get unconfirmed?" he said. "You see, I've been walking
around the grounds and woods here with a friend, and he's helped me

to come up with a whole new viewpoint. God is really *in* nature. He's in the trees, the rocks, the sky and the birds. Mom, I just can't believe in that heavenly Father bit any more. I want to be unconfirmed!"

Johnny's discovery walking in the woods was not just an adolescent phase through which he might pass, but rather a change in the basic way he and others view their world. Such a change of basic assumptions about the ways in which people perceive and relate to reality calls attention to a wide cultural movement challenging historic Western theistic belief today. This chapter will attempt to show why a harmless walk in the woods might lead people like Johnny to embrace such a fundamental change in their world view.

Twilight of Western Thought

In the years just following the First World War, W. B. Yeats wrote a poem that became famous because it captured the mood of that period and foreshadowed great changes that were soon to occur. In the second stanza of "The Second Coming" he says,

Surely some revelation is at hand;
Surely the Second Coming is at hand.

This he concludes from the social turbulence he sees reflected in a breakdown of authority and a loss of cohesion and focus. He takes note of the beginnings of anarchy and the loss of innocence:

The best lack all conviction, while the worst
Are full of passionate intensity.

Finally there comes to his troubled mind the image of some new incarnation—half beast, half man. He closes the poem with a question:

Now I know
That twenty centuries of stony sleep
Were vexed to nightmare by a rocking cradle,
And what rough beast, its hour come round at last,
Slouches towards Bethlehem to be born?[1]

Underlying Yeats's imagery was a fundamental question: "Is the time right in the West for the emergence of a totally new religion?" The question tends to be asked repeatedly, especially at periods of major social upheaval or decay. In the second century A.D., the Emperor Julian, also known as Julian the Apostate, journeyed to Delphi to ask essentially the same question. He had labored to revive the ancient gods of the Greek pantheon and stem the tide of the new religion, Christianity. He feared that his efforts would end in failure, and so he inquired of the famous Oracle about the chances of his campaign's success. Rarely did the Oracle answer people directly, and this time it answered Julian with the following prophetic word: "The temple is destroyed, the priests are gone, the treasuries are plundered, and the curtain of mystery is torn down." Julian got the message: the Roman world, tired and disillusioned, was indeed ready for a new word. His efforts were doomed to failure. It was in fact the last oracle ever to come from Delphi.

Many people today sense that we have come full cycle. They believe that we are in the twilight of Western thought. Convinced that there are no longer any rational answers to the problem of existence, they are fundamentally opposed to all dogma, whether it comes from rational, scientific or religious sources. Allan Bloom, in his stunning indictment of American education entitled *The Closing of the American Mind,* says that one thing a professor can be absolutely certain of today is that almost every student entering the university believes that truth is relative. The one value that dominates all others is openness. "There is no enemy other than the man who is not open to everything."

Paradoxically, as Bloom explains, such openness masks a much more fundamental closedness to anything claiming to be good or true. Although a rationalist himself rather than a Christian, Bloom credits the loss of any consistent vision for the whole of things which this openness produces to the disappearance of the Bible from our personal and corporate life. Much of his book is a sustained negative answer to his opening question: "When there are no shared goals or vision of the public good, is the social contract any longer possible?"[2]

Because there is no absolute foundation for right and wrong, Bloom asserts that we are left with a new morality of "values" devoid of ethical imperatives. Citing this loss of consensus, Bloom claims that history has disappeared as a yardstick for any commonly agreed-upon precedents. The enemy in our modern era is objectivity, the granting of objective truth to words, ideas or values.

Response to this wave of disillusionment with the accepted categories of thought has been varied. Some, as Bloom points out, stave off the despair by retreating into private worlds and pursue personal peace and prosperity. Others find "meaning" in the iconoclastic destruction of accepted values or the pursuit of utopian goals through social revolution—though their number has greatly waned in recent years and might well have disappeared but for apartheid in South Africa, oppression in Latin America and the persistent threat of nuclear war. Behind much of this is the verdict which Camus put so succinctly: "Truth is a colossal bore"—by which he meant that human attempts to invest the universe with rational significance are a waste of time.

However, "nature abhors a vacuum," and it is at these times in history when people, uprooted from traditional ways of thinking, are particularly susceptible to the influx of new ideas. Many still remember when MacArthur called for missionaries to come to Japan following World War 2. He had found an immense spiritual hunger created by the loss of the war and the Emperor's renunciation of divine claims. Conditions were ripe for a new religious movement. Relatively few responded to his call. The result was the emergence within Japan of its newest religion, Soka Gakkai, which gained millions of converts and in the seventies built what is reputed to be the largest religious structure in the world.

The Age of Aquarius

Today sweeping disillusionment of intellectuals with objective answers, persistent social problems that seem to defy solution, perva-

sive and triumphant materialism, coupled with the apparent obsoles-
cence of the historic churches, have all helped to produce a generation which is eager to find approaches to reality quite different from
those on which Western society was built.

And so to many of these seekers it seemed natural to turn to the
ancient wisdom of the East. In doing so they have encountered
teachers who borrow freely from the East's rich heritage, but mingle
it with insights from the so-called human potential movement and the
psychedelic subculture of the sixties to produce a new kind of consciousness that appears to offer an exciting and radically different
approach to reality.

The New Age Movement (NAM), as this new approach is coming
to be called, is far from a united cult. Nor should it be seen as a
conspiracy to deliberately undermine the West and all its achievements. It is rather a mosaic of diverse people, including physicists,
feminists, environmentalists, therapists, writers, entertainers, theologians, artists, martial artists and even an astronaut! Its heroes include
household names like celebrities Shirley MacLaine, Yoko Ono and
John Denver along with other well-known people—Werner Erhard,
Richard Bach, Elisabeth Kübler-Ross, Carlos Castaneda, Gary Zukav,
Fritjof Capra, Norman O. Brown, Charles Reich, George Leonard,
Arthur Koestler, Herman Hesse, Theodore Roszak, plus a host of
gurus and cult leaders like the Maharishi Mahesh Yogi (TM), the
Maharaj Ji (Divine Light Mission) and L. Ron Hubbard (Scientology).

Despite its great diversity this movement has a number of common
characteristics. First is its essential mysticism. In his *Making of a Counter Culture,* Theodore Roszak saw a deep hunger for mystery, in a
world where technology and objectivity were almost totally dominant,
as the key to the newer consciousness. Blame for the lack of a sense
of mystery in the West, claims Morris Berman in *The Reenchantment
of the World,*[3] is traceable to Descartes and Newton, who broke the
world into two separate realms: us "in here" and objects "out there."
This subject/object dualism he and others claim has been the foun-

tainhead of all our other crises, and it is only with the recovery of the
perspective that the universe is alive and totally interrelated that we
will recover what he calls "participatory consciousness."

A second characteristic of the New Age Movement is its syncretism.
In Boston there is a commune professing to follow the teachings of
Thoreau, Emerson and Christ. Another one exalts Jesus, Satan and
Lucifer. Minds conditioned to think logically find this combination of
apparent opposites to be a denial of the law of contradiction. However, says the NAM, this is precisely the problem. The mind must be
reconditioned to think of how all things are interrelated. A modern
mystic like F. C. Happold writes: "To India was given the vision of the
spiritual foundation of the universe and the immanence of God in it;
to Palestine the vision of the significance of the material world and
of the historical process; to Greece the vision of order and reason.
Each of these visions of reality can be seen as complementary, each
as a fragment of the full truth, each supplementing the other. All are
necessary if one is to grasp the full significance of the Christ."[4]

A third characteristic of the NAM is its blending of spirituality with
atheism. By this I mean that with the exception of Hare Krishna—
which contrary to other Hindu offshoots does have a place for a
personal God—virtually all New Age proponents join the East in rejecting the idea of one supreme, infinite God who is also at least as
personal as the creation he has made. With the Hindus they bid us
be totally silent about the nature of the supreme spirit. And with the
Buddhists they affirm an atheism that claims ultimate Reality to be
totally beyond the realm of the finite intellect.

The most famous Hindu saying comes from the Chandogya Upani-
shad[5] and says *Tat tvam asi*. Literally translated this means "That thou
art." This idea, meaning "you are god," is fundamental to Eastern
thought. Another famous equation declares "atman is Brahman"—or,
the soul of everyman is ultimate reality. Sometimes this takes the form
of pantheism (God is *everything,* and everything is god), and at other
times it takes the form of modified pantheism (God is *in* everything,

God is the principle behind nature). But either way this conception of reality depersonalizes God and makes him (or rather it) a part of the universe, denying what theologians call his transcendence. Theism on the other hand is the belief in one, personal, supreme, infinite God who is distinct from his creation and not simply a part of it.

In *Out on a Limb* actress Shirley MacLaine recounts her conversion from agnosticism to belief in the spirit realm. ABC heralded her discovery by creating a five-hour, two-part miniseries, exposing millions to her personal odyssey. The most basic spiritual law, says MacLaine, with all the energy of an evangelist, is this: "Everyone is God. Everyone."

Background

Philosophically the New Age Movement has its roots in what is known as monism. Starting with the assumption that there is only one essential principle in the cosmos, it concludes that despite apparent diversity all things are destined ultimately to merge into One. For some, whom we might call absolute monists, God is all there is. Everything else is illusion. For others, modified monists, God relates to matter as a soul does to the body. To the latter nature is not illusion; it is just not important.[6] To absolute monists salvation consists in escape from illusion; to modified monists it consists in merging one's self with nature and discovering the essential harmony of the two.

Over against this, theism starts with the assumption that since God created the universe the two, while related, must be kept distinct. Our ultimate goal as humans is neither escape from nor harmony with nature, but rather the recovery of a personal relationship with the God of nature. Whereas monists think in terms of merging, absorption and comingling, theists think in terms of relationship, reconciliation and fellowship. Monism's categories are impersonal, whereas theism's are personal.

Philosophic Tension

History yields abundant illustration of the basic incompatibility of

monism and theism. The Canaanite religion with which the Old Testament prophets were in continual tension, while ostensibly poly-
theistic, so identified God with the processes of nature that on a
philosophic level it must be considered monistic. It was because the
prophet Elijah encountered God, not in the wind, earthquake or fire,
but rather in the "still small voice," that he was strengthened to stand
against the prevailing Canaanite hegemony and emerge victorious.
The personal, holy God who was distinguishable from nature and
revealed himself as righteous was incompatible with a religion which,
for instance, sanctified ritual prostitution as a means toward the goal
of greater fertility. Archaeological evidence has also confirmed the
long-held suspicion of child sacrifice. In the name of Yahweh, these
prophets called the people away from the Canaanite fertility cult to
personal integrity and social justice.

Another example might be the mystery cults of the Greek world.
Although they began with a lofty contemplation of the heavens, they
ended in a kind of Faustian immersion in the hot blood of sacrificed
bulls. It was from a background similar to this that many converts
came into the early church in their hunger for lasting forgiveness and
the sure promise of eternal life.

Later, in the third century, Neo-Platonism again taught that God
could only be known by a mystical submersion of the individual in
the Absolute. Once again, while Neo-Platonists like Plotinus (205-270)
found a hearing within the church, Christian apologists opposed this
mysticism, claiming that God had revealed himself in history through
the Incarnation and could only be known through faith in Jesus
Christ.

One of the most striking twentieth-century examples of this age-old
conflict to which we might point was the opposition of certain Christians to the religious pretensions of Nazism. Amazing as it seems in
retrospect, there were philosophers and even theologians who had
permitted the identification of Aryanism with the divine spirit in such
a way that many people in the 1930s—even church people—thought

of Nazism as a kind of spiritual movement. But Karl Barth, in May of 1934, wrote the Barmen Confession, thus articulating for the so-called Confessing Church a theological basis upon which to stand against the religious pretentions of the Nazi movement.

Alfred Rosenberg, in his *Myth of the Twentieth Century*, traces many of the ideas of the Nazis back to the fourteenth-century German mystic Eckhart. Closer to hand, twentieth-century American expatriate poet Ezra Pound made a pilgrimage from Presbyterianism through sexual liberation to mysticism to the occult and eventually to Italian Fascism and Nazism. Having broken with his Christian past, he developed a theory that the secret of genius was to be found in a unique relationship between the testes and the pineal gland. Pressure from the one injected wisdom into the other. Living in Paris in the 1920s he was able to test this theory that sex, creativity and mysticism were all interwoven by engaging in numerous affairs and also by incorporating them in his poetry. Sex and eventually art became divinized. "One comes to the divine *through* the senses; by refining the emotions . . . one could receive revelations of divine truth."[7] Pound's Paris years were characterized by an increasing interest in astrology and the occult, undergirded by a monist philosophic outlook. The universe, as he saw it, was a vortex, "a system of energies that is unified at some mysterious point."[8] What attracted Pound to Fascism was its nonrational, intuitive, direct apprehension of truth, and its sense of an aristocracy of intellect and the arts. Pound's elitism prevented him from seeing what was happening right in front of his eyes, and long after other intellectuals abandoned Nazism, Pound was still signing letters with the swastika and closing them with "Heil Hitler, yrs. Ez."

Herman Hesse

Hesse's writings, perhaps more than those of any other Western writer, point out the implications of taking monism to its logical extreme. Virtually all his works breathe with this desire to unify all opposites and dissolve particulars in one universal. In *Demian* we see how the need to provide a truly unifying system that will integrate the dark, evil, devilish and sinister side of life with the bright, good side of life leads Hesse to present us with a monistic god that is both good and evil. His name for this god: Abraxis. Into this unifying deity go all the polarities of life: guilt and innocence, male and female, horror and delight, animalistic sex and sublime love.

The brilliance of Hesse's literary skill should never be allowed to blind us to the logic of his assumption: Abraxis demands that all things be incorporated into the divine nature—an Albert Schweitzer, on the one hand, and an Auschwitz and Buchenwald, on the other!

East Meets West: Marketing Monism

"East is East, and West is West, and never the twain shall meet." So thought Rudyard Kipling in the days before TV, jet travel, immigration, the UN and McDonalds! Today Western technology and culture is imported by the East, while Eastern gurus by the dozens crisscross North America in search of converts. Christianity grows at breakneck speed in the Third World, while residents of Wilmette, Illinois, drive past a Bahai temple on their way to their offices in the Chicago Loop.

The media has marketed the New Age Movement not only in TV specials, but in the new fascination with spirituality represented by films like *Close Encounters of the Third Kind, Cocoon,* even *Star Wars* where the Force that animates the cosmos and dwells within must be used against hostile powers in the universe. The fusion of sci-fi with the NAM is common. There are also a host of films dealing directly with the occult.

The drug experience gave enormous impetus to the NAM in its earlier phases during the 1960s. Timothy Leary's experiments with LSD, Aldous Huxley's experiences with mescaline, recorded in glowing terms in *Doors of Perception,* Ken Kesey's celebrations of acid trips with his "Merry Pranksters," Carlos Castaneda's out-of-the-body experiences on peyote or jimson weed, moving him beyond the psychedelic into the realm of sorcery—all these and others were justified in their day as part of a necessary breakthrough into higher consciousness.

The climax scene in the film *Easy Rider*, released in 1969, brought it all together. The scene takes place in a New Orleans cemetery. While the cameras simulate an LSD trip, powerful images of sex and death bombard the eyes, while in the background a child recites the Apostles' Creed. In this "total experience," religion, drugs, sex and death are all finally united.

But is this all really so new? Haven't we always had antirational philosophers like Spinoza and Rousseau who felt that the civilizing effects of reason were the real enemies of personal freedom? Haven't we always had mystics like William Blake who sought to see a

World in a grain of sand,

And Heaven in a wild flower?

And haven't there been many romantic aesthetes like Keats, for whom beauty is truth and truth is beauty, who would cry with him "O for a life of sensations rather than thoughts!"? The pendulum between rationalism and romanticism swings back and forth down the centuries across an abyss of nihilism. On the wall of a university dorm some graffiti humorously captured the swing from the sixties' emphasis on "action" to the seventies' on "introspection" to the eighties' on "intuition":

To do is to be—Sartre

To be is to do—Spinoza

Do be do be do—Sinatra

But while there have always been exponents of these differing emphases, what is new is the extraordinary appeal of the new consciousness today. Therefore before we respond to it we must try to understand why it manages to hold such an attraction for so many.

Five Benefits and Five Questions

The first appeal of the New Age Movement is its *unitive* concern. It seems to provide a principle of unification in the midst of a highly pluralistic world. One person who joined Bahai from a deeply Protestant background told me he did so because he hated making distinctions, having to exclude people and draw circles which left people out. Many like him wish there were ways of transcending the old distinctions of black and white, East and West, north and south, rich and poor, Protestant-Catholic-Jew, male and female. Meher Baba, a kindly guru with a small, devoted following in the sixties, appealed to this hunger when he said: "I have come to sow the seed of love in your hearts so that in spite of all superficial diversity which your life-in-illusion must experience and endure, the feeling of Oneness through love is brought about amongst all nations, creeds, sects and castes of the world."

But for all its attractiveness as an effort to overcome cleavages, we must ask a very basic question at this point. Doesn't the emphasis on oneness over against uniqueness eventually lead to the loss of our own uniqueness? How does the individual, with all his or her specialness, avoid being dissolved into the final, impersonal Absolute? If this be salvation, then it is a salvation by annihilation.

Second, the NAM is *spiritual.* By this I mean that it seems to offer an answer to the oppressive materialism that reduces all questions of value to the dollar. To many, Western religion has made an unholy alliance with materialism, and churches are in the business of selling their souls to pay off their mortgages. Devotees of the new consciousness counter this with a new focus on "inwardness."

When Harvey Cox pointed out psychological reasons for the drift Eastward in his book *Why Young Americans Are Buying Oriental Religions,* one respondent to a *Psychology Today* review said: "The eminence of his credentials makes one wonder whether the reductionism once confined to the Freudians ("religion is nothing but . . . ") has now seeped into Western theology to such an extent that those seeking genuine spiritual inspiration have little choice but to turn Eastward."[9]

After astronaut Edgar D. Mitchell walked on the moon in February

1971, he returned, evaluated his experience and opted for the NAM. "The value-free rational-objective-experimental mode of Western science, based on (philosophic) materialism is not sufficient by itself for coping with the ever-increasing planetary crises besetting civilization. The intuitive-subjective-experiential mode characteristic of religion and Eastern traditions has much to contribute to the study of mind and consciousness."[10] The NAM feeds on this unnecessary antithesis.

But whether antimaterialism takes the form of rejecting objectivity for subjectivity (Theodore Roszak in *Where the Waste Land Ends,* 1972) or rejecting technocracy for consciousness (Charles Reich in *The Greening of America,* 1970) or espousing esoteric forms of mysticism (Carlos Castaneda in *Journey to Ixtlan,* 1972), this attack on what is considered the one-dimensional character of Western materialism implies a rejection of the value of matter itself. If the West can be accused of "killing" humankind by turning them into machines, can the East not also "kill" humankind by turning them into a soul or a mind—beings who find value only by denying a very important part of who they are, namely their bodies?

Then there are many who are tired of absolutes or convinced that in an age exalting personal choice there ought not to be any imperatives in the area of ethics. These find a third feature of the NAM appealing: its *relativism.* It is, of course, quite impossible to make distinctions in the area of ethics when your god is a composite of good and evil. When words like *love, sharing, freeing, self-transcending* are used by New Age devotees, there is no way of spelling out what these words mean in terms of specifics. Any action can conceivably be loving or freeing or self-transcending. As everything is ultimately judged by one's own awareness or perception, these words can mean almost anything.

In Hesse's *Siddhartha* the logic of this relativism becomes clear when at the end of his life Siddhartha (who is the Buddha) concludes:

Everything that exists is good—death as well as life, sin as well as holiness, wisdom as well as folly. Everything is necessary, every-

eds only my agreement, my assent, my loving understand-ing: then all is well with me and nothing can harm me. I learned through my body and soul that it was necessary for me to sin, that I needed lust, that I had to strive for property and experience nausea and the depths of despair in order to learn not to resist them, in order to learn to love the world, and no longer compare it with some kind of desired imaginary world, some imaginary vi-sion of perfection, but to leave it as it is, to love it and be glad to belong to it.[11]

This sounds beautiful, but where is there any direction for a personal or a social ethic? Why should one wage a war on poverty? prejudice? apartheid? cancer? ignorance? hunger? A true Easterner would most likely answer that doing good creates good karma (fate/destiny), and doing evil creates bad karma. Therefore it is better to do good. But this only shows how even in the East the people never took monism to its logical end as Hesse did. Writing for intellectuals and not the masses, Hesse tried to make of moral relativism something beautiful and poetic. He wasn't as concerned about "right and wrong" as he was about "good and evil"—in other words, the merging of cosmic forces into a unified whole. But the question still stands, given a monistic philosophic foundation, why should anybody try to change anything for the better?

A fourth reason for the appeal of the New Age Movement is its appearance of *bringing science and spirituality together.* It has spawned a whole new vocabulary of scientific-sounding words that link "con-sciousness" with objective research.

John W. White, author of three books on the consciousness revo-lution, cites thirteen frontiers where consciousness research is being done: (1) altered states of consciousness (for example, dreams and trances accessible through drugs and hypnosis), (2) biofeedback (for example, brain wave control), (3) body consciousness (for example, karate, kung fu, acupuncture and other body/mind therapies), (4) exobiology (for example, study of extraterrestrial forms of life, UFOlogists), (5) linguistics (for example, metalinguistics, psycholinguistics, transformational grammar, and the various ways brain waves affect language), (6) meditation research, (7) metapsychiatry (for example, the interface between psychiatry and psychic-mystic experiences), (8) neuroscience (for example, orthodox brain research that may come up with unorthodox conclusions), (9) paraphysics (for example, the physics of paranormal processes), (10) psychic research (for example, mediumship and ways "consciousness can operate externally to the body"), (11) reality studies (for example, how our understanding of "reality" is shaped by perception, cultural conditioning and mind games), (12) thanatology (for example, research into the process of death and dying) and (13) transpersonal psychology (for example, how to help people develop to their fullest potential through peak experiences, ecstasy and psychotechnologies).[12]

For a number of years writers like Arthur Koestler, Laurence Le-Shan and William Irwin Thompson have attempted to point to the corollaries between psychic phenomena and modern physics. The most recent, and probably the most widely read addition to this list, is Fritjof Capra. An Austrian physicist currently living in Berkeley, California, Capra, in his most popular book *The Tao of Physics,* tries to show that the physics of subatomic particles as developed by Einstein, Planck and Heisenberg has exploded the idea of "hard" matter and has shown that these particles are "abstractions" observable only through their interrelationship with other systems. The book tries to claim that this brings modern physics and mysticism together, for "the observer and the observed" are now inseparable. The subject/object dichotomy has been overcome. Later books by Capra have tried to translate this into a game plan for the transformation of approaches to psychology, economics, medicine and biology and then to a "whole earth catalogue" of social changes.

Aside from the fact that scientists on the whole seem unimpressed, and even the most sympathetic among them worry that if the future of mysticism is tied to physics it might, like the science it is linked to, need constant revision and updating,[13] a fundamental question remains. Why, if the goal of mysticism is inner peace, does Capra with his crusading zeal disturb the status quo to *spread* his new vision of the world? In other words, the religious traditions on which he draws are conspicuously unconcerned for social change. In fact John R. Miles, editor of the University of California Press, asks what "ought" caused Capra even to descend from the heights of enlightenment into the depths of the publishing business long enough to write his books?[14] It is the absence of any place for a moral imperative within the monistic system that forces one to raise this question.

A fifth appeal of the NAM is its *holistic* approach to problems. To devotees reality is a seamless web of vibrant, pulsating energy. Putting together an intuitive means of knowing, a feminine spirituality derived from a new nurturing image of the deity, and a wide variety of techniques for applying "enlightenment" to everything from business decisions to nutrition would create a new social order.

The question is: will it? As Robert Burrows writes: "The vision [that Capra believes will deliver us] seems to thrive in cultures where misery is perpetually rampant and corruption rife. India is a case in point. Christians know that the problem is human perversity, not human perception—holiness, not holism."[15]

Abandoning Transcendence

Should it surprise us that Western people hungering for an experience of transcendence have not turned in greater numbers to Christianity? Were they to do so, what would they discover? On the one hand, they would encounter a liberal form of Christianity that has abandoned transcendence for a view of God totally bounded by a closed system. A generation ago names like Paul Tillich and John A. T. Robinson paved the way for the subsequent brief but notable "death of God" movement by identifying God with the "ground of being." God's supremacy over nature was completely abandoned for a vision of God's presence "within the depths." Although Tillich and

Robinson used Christian terminology, the historic Incarnation, Cross and Resurrection of Jesus had no essential place in their theology.

They were calling Christendom to a "Copernican revolution" in theology, a discovery of the transcendent within the immanent. Of course, German theology had been doing that for more than a century in its fascination with the religious consciousness of a non-supernatural Jesus, but Robinson sought to bring this to the level of the ordinary churchman. In doing so he tried to distinguish what he called his "immanentist" world view from mere pantheism by insisting on a personal, loving, free ground to all Reality rather than pantheism's impersonal, uncaring, deterministic one.[16] But the graft wouldn't take. Within a very short time a generation of radical theologians had taken Robinson's and Tillich's denial of transcendence to its logical extreme and proclaimed the "death of God."

Their theological heirs greet the New Age Movement with enthusiasm for while it uses Eastern rather than Western "myths," it moves in the same direction: inwardness combined with what appears to be an egalitarian social ethic.[17] In a review of Capra's *The Turning Point* in *Theology*, a liberal Protestant scholarly journal, the reviewer never once questions Capra's pantheism, but rather hails the book with the following words: "At a time when science and religion are finding themselves on convergent courses in their common search for truth, Capra has provided a panoramic view of the terrain. . . . Here is a sense of poetic wonder at the lively intricacies of the evolving universe in which mankind is privileged to play a creative role."[18] The same sort of breathless enthusiasm for immanence underlies the reception given by the liberal clergy to Martin Sorcese's pantheistic recreation of Jesus in the film *The Last Temptation of Christ*.

On the other hand, should these same people turn to the conservative churches in their search, they face a different but strangely parallel dilemma: Many of the more conservative churches have lost the very sense of mystery for which the present generation is starved. John Stott laments: "We evangelicals do not know much about worship. . . . We have little sense of the greatness of Almighty God. . . . The secular experience of transcendence constitutes a powerful challenge to the quality of our Christian public worship."[19]

But where can modern people really find answers to the hunger they feel for that which is ultimate, for something or someone who can lift them beyond the seductive materialism that announces "Coke's the Real Thing"? If the East's wisdom fails to provide an adequate basis for either a personal or a social ethic and neither the NAM nor the new theology get us far enough outside our own subjectivity to build a bridge to Truth, is there somewhere else to go?

Liberating Truth

As Meredith stepped into my office, I wondered how this calm, attractive young woman in her late twenties could know much about the world of spiritual phenomena. How wrong I was! Her story read like a page out of Edgar Cayce.

At a young age, Meredith began searching for truth. It soon became a way of life. Once away from the protective cocoon of her family and into university, she began to explore the unconscious in earnest. Beginning with psychology courses, she was soon into the heavier stuff: Castenada, Hesse, Nietzsche and especially Jung. Catapulted into the world of eastern mysticism, it wasn't long before she crossed the line into the murky world of the occult. She did tarot cards and est, attended courses on "self-healing" at an institute in Toronto, and developed her own form of meditation. She searched for oneness with everything, including the dark, evil side of nature.

Through the influence of some Christian friends, Meredith was exposed to Christ in a fresh and vital way. While she was interested in what they shared with her, she still felt constrained by spiritual forces she could not explain.

At a New Age bookstore she came in contact with a man who claimed to be a psychic and who took her under his wing. Gradually he began to assert absolute control over her. He urged her to join him in listening to "voices from hell" on a taped recording. He kept her up late at nights admitting things from her past. He claimed to have experienced out-of-the-body states like astral projection. Gradually, he separated her from all her friends and family, and Meredith realized that she was caught. Her mentor watched her like a hawk, never letting her out of the house with her purse, lest she make an attempt to leave. Finally, thanks to the intervention of her brother, she escaped, leaving everything behind except a credit card and some letters.

Slowly, because of her past fears, Meredith has entered the Christian fellowship and now confesses Christ. There was a look of peace on her face as she told me that she now feels free. I asked her where she felt she went wrong. "I think it began with an excessive desire to please, which made me susceptible to persuasive teachers." One thing of which she is now certain: the freedom she feels is directly related to the gracefulness of a God who does not abandon her to subjectivity, that is to the exhausting task of creating her own truth, but has revealed himself to her as a truth-telling God.

Turning Aside to See

Tracing the roots of the Judeo-Christian understanding of God (and, for that matter, the Islamic understanding as well) takes us back in history to an experience Moses had in the desert. In the book of Exodus we learn that Moses, having fled Egypt, settled in the desert and by marriage joined himself to the house of Jethro, priest of Midian.

Although brought up in the royal house of Egypt, Moses came to discover to his chagrin that he was not an Egyptian but actually a Hebrew by birth. As the tension between these increasingly hostile peoples had grown too strong, he was finally forced to choose between the established powers, on the one hand, and the despised slaves, on the other. Moses took the fast road to Midian.

At this point in his life, as far as he knew he was to remain a permanent fixture in Jethro's house. No passion to save his people burned within his soul. No vision of a promised land to lead his people toward, and no burning concern for the law of God motivated him. He was content where he was.

But a dramatic event in Moses' life changed all this, and in time this event altered the history of the world. Moses had an encounter with God one day in the desert. Within months of this event he would stand before the king of Egypt and demand: "Let my people go!" He would then be caught up in one of history's greatest political and religious confrontations. Because of this Moses would be remembered for all time as the man who liberated a nation, not with the weapons of war, but by the sheer exercise of moral and spiritual power.

It all happened at a burning bush. Moses saw that a bush was aflame, but was not being consumed. Not an ordinary bush caught by the rays of the setting sun, nor one of the brilliant flowering variety that are occasionally found in that territory, this was an ordinary bush, literally on fire with the presence of God. When Moses turned aside to see, he was told: "Take off your shoes from your feet, for the place on which you are standing is holy ground."

God and Nature

By the choice of this means of revelation to Moses, God was saying something important about his interaction with the natural order. Had the bush been consumed, God would have been saying that he was totally transcendent over nature. Nature is consumed by his presence and power. But had this been just an ordinary, beautiful bush that was not really on fire but merely a vehicle for "revelation" to Moses, God would have been saying that he was totally immanent in nature. Elizabeth Barrett Browning expressed this latter view beautifully when she wrote:

Earth's crammed with heaven.
And every common bush afire with God;
But only he who sees takes off his shoes.
The rest sit round it and pluck blackberries.[20]

Had the bush appeared to Moses other than as Exodus tells it, the biblical understanding of God would have been radically different. Had the bush really been consumed, the biblical God would have been like the gods of the Greek pantheon, transcendent but not immanent. From the top of Mt. Olympus these gods hurled thunderbolts down to earth. The world was their playground. But had the bush been merely a "common bush," and the point of the story that Moses had had an unusual enlightenment, then the biblical God would have been totally immanent but not transcendent—a presence within nature discovered by those who turn aside and see. In either case the natural world would have been relatively unimportant; either because it was transcended by that which was above it or because it was eclipsed by that which was within it. Or else God would be unimportant, because he would be an outcropping of nature.

What Moses in fact experienced was a real, objective God, who had sanctified nature and made it a vehicle through which he could encounter both his transcendence and his immanence. Both dimensions of God later reflected themselves in Moses' character. His immanence shone through Moses' divinely inspired leadership, while his transcendence could be seen in the depth of Moses' humility. For Moses, one of history's great leaders, was remembered as "the meekest man in all the earth."[21]

In this transforming experience Moses discovered three aspects of God that have ever since been formative of our understanding of the God whom Jesus called Father.

First, he discovered that this is indeed *a God who speaks.* In contrast to the eternal silence of the gods of the East, this God chose as his special people a group of Semitic Near Eastern tribes and turned them into what Theodore Roszak called "the greatest listeners in history." No other people had discovered what their leader Moses did: that God speaks to them from outside and communicates his will to them in ways that are both intelligible and personal.

Subsequent biblical history continues to reveal that God breaks in with a word. Through prophets, men and women of wisdom, angels, and supremely through his Son, Jesus, and the Apostles he chose and trained, the word breaks in. This is quite a different process than that whereby perceptive souls embark on a search which eventually brings them to the truth. On the contrary, it is a process of being amazed and stunned at what we see and hear. It is not a process of observing God; it is the opposite, being observed by him. It is being summoned by his Word.

The second aspect of God that Moses discovered was that the biblical God is *a God who saves.* He hears the cry of his people and sees their affliction. He comes to their aid and delivers them from their oppressors.

Biblical people insist that all authentic knowledge of God has its roots in God's act of deliverance. To know God is always to know one's deliverer from oppression. The voice from the bush reminded Moses that he was encountering "the God of Abraham, Isaac and Jacob." God was not new, not different from the God of his fathers. God was the same. So, when Jesus called this God his "Father" (using undeniably masculine imagery, but not thinking of God as a man) and when Christians down the ages speak of God, we recognize the God of Moses and Abraham as our own.

God never ceases to be a deliverer because, according to Judeo-Christian teaching, our fundamental problem is bondage. Throughout Israel's history and supremely in the death of Christ on the cross and his resurrection, God goes on delivering. Political deliverance is simply an outworking of a deeper moral and spiritual deliverance. In this knowledge believers find freedom from the power and penalty of sin as well as a call to join in the task of freeing all who experience oppression.

Finally, Moses encountered *a God who sends.* Mission is always inherent in the knowledge of God. In the oft-quoted words of Emil Brunner: "The Church exists by mission as fire exists by burning." While there is an honored place for meditation and the reflective disciplines within Christianity, there is no place for a passivity that is not linked with mission. St. Teresa of Avila is remembered as a contemplative, but she was a preacher and a reformer; Mother Teresa is known as an activist, but the popular press often forgets that her work flows from a deep contemplative spiritual discipline. The two rightly belong together.

Situated on the campus of Yale University is the Beinicke Rare Book Library, a collection of some of the most ancient and valuable books in the world. In front of it lies an impressive sunken garden, reflecting a world view that I suspect is shared by very few of the authors of the books gathered in that great collection. In the garden, which is made entirely of marble, crisscross lines like those on a Mercator projection map simulate the universe. In one corner is a large marble pyramid, symbolizing time. In another corner is a huge doughnut-shaped structure standing on its side. It symbolizes energy. Then in a third corner, perched precariously on one tip is a huge die just about to topple this way or that. This is the symbol of chance. What the visitor sees is a representation of the world view of modern man: a self-existing universe consisting of energy, time and chance. In such a view of the world, the individual feels small and of little significance, his destiny is simply to be a part of blind, uncaring fate.

Both the New Age Movement, with its Eastern monistic underpinning, and biblical faith rebel against this deterministic Absolute. The one turns within in an attempt to discover the mystical unity of all things. The other looks beyond to a Creator, Redeemer and Initiator. It is up to us to discover which "dream" is true. But one thing is certain, we must start with ourselves, with our longing for significance, with our struggles with good and evil, not only in society but in our own wills, and with that unique combination of feeling and intellect that make up our natures. Can ultimate Reality force us to deny what we already know?

It was A.D. 32 and Jesus faced a barrage of accusers at the Feast of Dedication which was in full swing in Jerusalem. Infuriated by the blasphemy of his claim to be the Son of God, they challenged him. In responding to them Jesus chose what to our modern ears, untrained in the methods of Rabbinic debate, sounds like a very strange way of pointing out that they were on shaky ground. Quoting to them a portion of Psalm 82, he said: "Is it not written in your law, 'I said, you are gods'? If he called them gods to whom the word of God came (and scripture cannot be broken), do you say of him whom the Father consecrated and sent into the world, 'You are blaspheming,' because I said, 'I am the Son of God'?"[22]

His reply had a double edge to it. Just as in Psalm 82 God had been denouncing the judges of Israel for failing to judge righteously in their day, Jesus chided the leaders of Israel for not recognizing him for who he was. But he was also making a very subtle point. Jesus was saying look at how great the people whom God calls his own are! They are gods—or at least sons of God. All they did to deserve that wonderful description was simply receive God's word. He made them his sons, and even called them "gods." How then can I be blaspheming when I say I am the Son of God? That was a show-stopper. Jesus was saying that their failure to recognize him had its roots in their low view of themselves. Jesus uncovered their fundamental problem. We are so small, they thought, why would God deign to come down to our level and reveal himself in such a personal and compassionate way as Jesus was doing? Jesus was saying, in effect: "Look how great you are, what wonderful creatures of God you are, and then look at the character of God in the light of this reality."

In just such a way we must hold on to the significance of who we are and begin with a resolute determination neither to dissolve our identity into the impersonal, mystical Absolute nor to surrender our rationality to a one-sided intuitive, elite path to insight, but rather to listen to the still small voice that addresses us as whole people.

Not far from the Beinecke Library is a simple lead fountain in honor of a graduate who in the 1930s turned his back on a huge dairy fortune in order to set out as a missionary for Jesus Christ. Bill Borden had "turned aside to see," he had heard a word addressed to him, and then, liberated from all that bound him, he sought to share his knowledge of an infinite and personal God. If people today would take the short walk from the Beinecke garden to the Borden fountain, they would find not only God but themselves as well.

And Pharaoh said to Joseph, "Say to your brothers, 'Do this: load your beasts and go back to the land of Canaan; and take your father and your households, and come to me, and I will give you the best of the land of Egypt, and you shall eat the fat of the land.'" *(GENESIS 45:17-18)*

3

View from Pharaoh's Porch
The Humanist's Refusal

IT WAS A BEAUTIFUL SPRING DAY. THE DOGWOODS SCAT-
tered throughout the rolling green campus of this prestigious New
England boarding school added a lacy touch to the backdrop of fresh-
ly mowed lawns and stately Georgian buildings. The chapel, with its
tall spire dominating the campus, was no longer used for compulsory
services, but still served as a handsome memorial to all of the virtues
on which the school had been founded and a comfort to prospective
parents uneasy about releasing their sons and daughters to this un-
familiar environment.

In the marble entrance hall to the administration building, busts of
John F. Kennedy and Adlai Stevenson impressed visitors with the
succession of illustrious graduates whose boyhood years were shaped
by the Ivy-League-educated faculty and the two clergyman headmas-
ters, father and son, who had left their mark on the school.

Into my office on the third floor strode a lad I had never seen
before, but he apparently knew that our small organization, FOCUS

(The Fellowship of Christians in Universities and Schools)—which happened to have been based at his school, thanks to the headmaster's encouragement—was unapologetically Christian.

Ted, as I later learned he was named, decided to skip over what seemed to him unnecessary introductions in order to get straight to his point. "What do you say to someone who cannot believe?" he shot at me.

One didn't expect such straightforwardness from the sons and daughters of America's Establishment—and I knew them pretty well, having founded FOCUS with the explicit aim of Christianizing them! So Ted's challenge, thinly disguised in the form of a question, deserved a careful answer.

"What is it you can't believe?" I replied.

"I can't believe in miracles, in Virgin Births, in heaven and hell. But those are only part of the picture. I can't believe in your personal, supernatural God."

I studied Ted's young face. He hardly seemed old enough to have wrestled with the deeper questions of life. But his carriage gave me to believe that he had prepared himself well to confront his first professionally religious person. I was to learn subsequently that he was one of the school's brightest students and headed for Harvard in the fall.

"Well, then," I replied, "tell me what you can believe."

Without flinching, he came back with the following credo: "I believe in the infinite perfectibility of human nature."

In good Rogerian fashion I restated his position, while pondering how to respond: "You believe, then, that people are getting better and better all the time, and eventually they will reach some kind of moral perfection where they can live in a utopia?"

When Ted said "Yes," I asked another question: "Do you have any evidence that you can point to that we are in fact getting better and better all the time?" Ted thought for a minute. "No, but I still believe it."

Trying to clarify where we were, I then said: "You have just told me

that you have a faith for which you have no evidence." While 1 ...
absorbed that, I invited him to sit down with me and look through
some of the evidence I might show him for what it was I believed. But
his time had run out, and just as quickly as he had appeared, he left.

While Ted might have resisted the label, he was a young and bud-
ding humanist. His views coincided perfectly with those who would
advocate humanism as the only tenable world view today. From the
media to the classroom and even, in some cases, to the pulpit, humanism permeates our culture and penetrates our lives. Kodak captured the
essence of humanism with the theme of its fascinating exhibit at Walt
Disney World's EPCOT Center: "If you can dream it, you can do it."

The Humanist Manifesto

Like every movement, the humanist movement has its hard core. In
1933 some thirty-four noted scholars published *The Humanist Manifesto*. Then again in 1973 over one hundred ninety people, including
many renowned scholars, signed *The Humanist Manifesto II*. Studying
the list of names, I was somewhat surprised, but not completely, to
discover the name of one of my former seminary professors among
them! Humanism encompasses a very broad spectrum indeed, and
today in the Western world it is one of the primary alternatives to
religious faith.

As a group humanists are defined by their criticisms of religion—
especially of historic Christian faith—and by a set of assumptions that
they substitute for those of the Bible. Both bear careful examination.

Humanists say that Christians have the wrong focus. Not all humanists go as far as the German philosopher Friedrich Nietzsche, who
proclaimed "God is dead." But all would agree that if he is not, he
is at the very least irrelevant. To view the world through God-con-
scious spectacles is, according to a humanist, to get the whole human
enterprise out of focus. As Pythagoras, the ancient Greek philosopher,
said, "man is the measure of all things." And if this is so, then Alex-
ander Pope, writing in the eighteenth century, couldn't have put it

better when he said:

Know then thyself, presume not God to scan,
The proper study of mankind is man.

Modern humanists believe that humanity is autonomous. We are totally on our own. We do not have at our disposal any standards of measurement by which to evaluate what we see around us, save those which our own reason perceives. The past president of the British Humanist Association, H. J. Blackham, writes that nothing can be exempt from human questioning, and that no tradition, authority, inside knowledge or axioms can be used as a standard for interpreting our own experience. Only experience can interpret further experience, and in the process all standards must be completely open to question and revision.[1]

Although some might find it confining to limit one's study only to those things which people can verify through their own experience, the humanist points to the fact that our knowledge of all subjects doubles about every ten years. Yesterday's textbooks are soon out of date. Tomorrow's will be substantially different from today's. To whom do we owe all this new knowledge about our environment, our society, our psychology, art, history and ideas? To those, say humanists, who have made the proper study of humankind to be humans themselves. Nor is it a fact overlooked by humanists that in the humanities and in the sciences a sizeable number of department heads at our major universities are articulate humanists.

Turn Back, O Man of God

A second criticism of the Christian point of view shared by humanists is that it has a backward focus. Facing the past rather than the future, it cherishes outmoded ways and inhibits progress. *The Humanist Manifesto* said: "In place of the old attitudes involved in worship and prayer, the Humanist finds his religious emotions expressed in a heightened sense of personal life and in a cooperative effort to promote social well-being." Forty years later, in *The Humanist Manifesto*

II, this same point was echoed: "Humanists still believe that traditional theism, especially faith in the prayer-hearing God, assumed to love and care for persons, to hear and understand their prayers, and to be able to do something about them, is an unproved and outmoded faith. . . . Reasonable minds look to other means for survival. . . . Humanism offers an alternative that can serve present-day needs and guide humankind toward the future."

On the surface this criticism seems sound. Christians necessarily look backward to the Bible just as Americans look backward to the Constitution. Each document not only interprets the past, but shapes the present and guides the future. Without the ability to look backwards one soon loses one's way.

Some Christians have been so absorbed in the past that they have been unable to face or influence the future. Critics of missionary practices often justifiably point to the harmful effects on primitive cultures of naive, though well-meaning, missionaries, who have been as zealous at covering the natives' bare breasts as they have been at converting their lost souls!

However, it is from digesting the past that we gain both a vision and the energy to shape the future. And it is only as that vision is deeply rooted in our souls that we are able to have an impact on our world. As G. K. Chesterton argued, as long as the vision of "heaven" is always changing, the vision of "earth" will remain the same. Those who continually change their minds will never change their world. It is because the dreams of the Mother Teresas and the Martin Luther Kings arise out of the depths of the past—the specifically Christian past—that their message captures the hearts and mobilizes the energies of millions, just as in the nineteenth century William Wilberforce's biblical piety was the well-spring of his successful campaign to end slavery.

Modern Africa not long ago seemed prepared to shake off Christianity along with the shackles of colonialism. But today demographers predict that at the present rate of church growth, all of sub-

Sahara Africa will be Christian by the year 2000. Why the change? Africa has observed that it has been the Christians—both black and white—who have cared, worked, built, educated, served and loved in the name of Christ. Africa is pinning its future to the Christian dream.

Humanism's confidence in science, while understandable in the light of the countless blessings that have come to the human race through science, strangely overlooks science's own origins in the biblical world view. Professor Alan Richardson and others have argued that modern science, with its emphasis on induction and experiment, could only have grown out of a post-Aristotelian, biblically influenced, world view where knowledge is acquired from observation rather than from "first principles."[2]

Early scientists like Kepler believed that they were "thinking God's thoughts after him," while Isaac Newton and Roger Bacon each claimed that their scientific studies grew out of their conviction that the world was God's and therefore worth studying for its own merits. It was really not until the eighteenth century that modern science was forcibly wrested from its roots in a biblical view of the world. Nor can it be claimed that science always moves civilization in the direction of wholeness and survival. Canadian science popularizer David Suzuki has pointed out that about half of all scientists are employed in military projects, while many others spend their time tormenting dogs to test cosmetics! As part of a wider dream science can make a grand contribution, but despite humanist claims, common sense knows that it can be either a friend or an enemy.

A third criticism which humanists make builds on the first two. Not only is the Christian focus on life misdirected and backward, it is, from the humanist point of view, positively harmful: "Salvationism, based on mere affirmation, still appears as harmful, diverting people with false hopes of heaven hereafter."[3] The apparently irrational nature of religious faith bothers humanists. Their system is built on reason. H. J. Blackham, in *Objections to Humanism*, rejects the application of the word *religion* to humanism. For him it is the lack of dogma that is humanism's real attraction. He says, "One of the fundamental positions taken by Humanists is that men should have freedom to think out for themselves how they ought to live, to think out their own principles."[4]

While Christians would want to question the claim, humanists assert that it is precisely because of irrational objections, based on religious scruples, to sex education in public schools that young American girls do not get the birth-control information that they need. "No wonder," say humanists, "America's rate of teen-age pregnancy is twice that of Europe's."

Before we form a Christian response, can we not feel at least on the surface some of the attractiveness of these arguments? There have been well-meaning believers who, like ostriches, have hidden their heads in the sand, not wanting to hear anything that might challenge their beliefs. When the wife of the bishop of Worcester heard the news in 1860 that man might have some distant relationship to the apes, she exclaimed: "Descended from apes! Let's hope it is not true, but if it is, let us pray that it will not become generally known."[5] Does the average Christian equip himself to face the challenges to his faith which modern society might bring? Dorothy Sayers, mystery writer and Christian apologist, once said: "The average Christian is about as ready to do battle with a convinced Marxist on the fundamentals of his faith as a boy with a pea shooter is facing a fanfare of machine guns."

Godlike Proportions

While I have no basis for questioning this, I do know it is of course quite illogical to assume that because humanists can score points against Christians, they are right in all that they affirm. H. L. Mencken, who was no friend of organized religion, wisely said: "The world always makes the assumption that the exposure of error is identical with the discovery of truth—that truth and error are simply opposites. They are nothing of the sort. What the world turns to, when it has been cured of one error, is usually simply another error and may be worse than the first." The humanists' affirmations must be examined as well as their denials.

Chief among humanists' cardinal beliefs is a deep reverence for humankind. They want to affirm the uniqueness, dignity and the ultimate worth of human beings without tying that belief to a Creator before whom all must bow and on whose pleasure our existence depends. As a neighbor lamented once to my wife about her son's new interest in Christianity: "We don't know what went wrong. We always brought him up to believe in his own significance. Now he seems to need a crutch."

To fill the vacuum left by an absent or nonexistent God, humanism's "man" has to achieve godlike proportions. From the premise that we have no one but ourselves to depend on—immortalized in William E. Henley's famous lines "I am the master of my fate: I am the captain of my soul"—humanists proceed to celebrate our mastery of our environment,[6] our ability to create our own values, our right to be our own judge and finally our role as sole savior of the human race.

As Os Guinness has shown in _The Dust of Death,_ the modern humanist speaks no longer in the rhapsodic tones of nineteenth-century writers like Algernon Charles Swinburne, who wrote the hymn "Glory to Man in the highest! for Man is the master of things," or in the hushed reverence of an Auguste Comte, who created a religion with a catechism, sacraments, priesthood and liturgy—all to the glory of the Great Being, whom he defined as humanity.[7] Today our deification is put in far less romantic and far more pragmatic terms, such as those of the late John F. Kennedy who is reputed to have said: "All men's problems were created by man, and can be solved by man." But the net effect is the same.

Humanism lauds humanity only to destroy it. Modern humanists, Herbert Schlossberg argues, displace God and exalt themselves, and thus repeat the age-old fallacy of thinking that good and evil can be known apart from submission to God's will. The result is an ethical system which locates good and evil subjectively in one's own perceptions. Good is what I perceive or feel to be good, and evil is the opposite. From this platform humanists make their plea not only for abortion on demand, but also for assisted suicide, the selective non-treatment of handicapped newborns and the destruction of the senile by euthanasia. Such actions, all explicitly condoned in *The Humanist Manifesto*, are, it is argued, for the good of those concerned.

Such conclusions, so offensive to many, flow naturally from the humanist premise that personhood is not something inherent in an individual and therefore sacred, but something conferred on those whom society deems valuable. Just as personhood is a judgment made in favor of the valuable, so it can be a judgment made against those not valuable. The senile, the retarded, along with the unwanted unborn can be denied personhood and eliminated at the will of others.

In a recent book, news correspondent Betty Rollin gives a detailed account of how she and her husband assisted her mother to commit suicide. The book, *Last Wish,* became a best seller and will soon be a feature film. Rollin's mother was struggling with ovarian cancer. She was depressed and in pain. She asked for assistance in dying. Betty Rollin and her husband decided that their role was not to reassure her mother of the preciousness of her life nor was it to work harder with the doctors for the control of her mother's pain, but rather to assist her in a speedy death. The book, which fails to deal with the moral issues involved, nonetheless has had a wide appeal because of the shock value of the story and the supposedly obvious benefit to Betty Rollin's mother in the speedy end to her miseries.

It should be noted that because there are no objective values to point to, it is just as easy for humanists to justify killing someone because of the benefit to *them* as it is to justify killing someone because of the apparent benefit to *others.* Could humanists not have justified killing Betty Rollin's mother because of the benefit to Betty Rollin and her husband? We rightly recoil at the suggestion. But, if life has no intrinsic value and is dependent for its value purely on the worth others place on it, then it is logically of no consequence to whose benefit another's death might be. Any action can be justified on the basis of one's feelings of what is right.

Persons Vs. Human Beings

It becomes quite natural to find humanists arguing that there is a fundamental difference between "persons" and "human beings." According to this reasoning, a human being does not become a person at conception, nor at "quickening," nor even at birth! Furthermore, a human being can cease being a "person" when someone else decides that they are no longer able to function as a full person. Michael Tooley argues that it is a "wild contention" to say that newborn babies are persons. There ought to be a three-day waiting period following birth during which the parents decide whether or not to confer personhood on their baby. In the event that they do not, the baby may be destroyed.[8]

Similarly, the infirm elderly may be destroyed—indeed ought to be, says Nobel Prize-winning biophysicist Francis Crick—if they are a drain on the younger generation or on limited resources. Crick believes it ought to be mandatory to put to death all persons over eighty—a point which will have increasing appeal to a smaller and smaller younger generation forced to support a larger aging one.[9] Nor is he alone in this idea. Another humanist argues that those suffering serious handicaps ought to be eliminated because of the hardships this causes to others.[10]

There is, of course, an inescapable logic about all this. Given the ultimate value which humanists place on human intelligence, it follows that those lacking in human intelligence are lacking in value. It is only a short step from this to the assertion that they have no value!

The dehumanizing effects of humanism's agenda for the poor is another point Schlossberg argues. By seeing the poor solely as victims and by advocating programs which tend to create further dependency rather than motivate toward self-help, well-meaning benefactors of the poor actually create a people who despise themselves. Such an attitude is traceable to a humanism which, while professing to exalt humanity, can only view humankind collectively rather than individually. Manipulative approaches to aiding the poor through increased organizational dependencies spring from the certainty that humanists have that they "know" that poor people have an inferior life.

While believers would want to insist that only God can evaluate the significance of a person's life, humanists have no judgment beyond their own. Therefore, what they see to be good for another must be final. That is why the Danish philosopher Søren Kierkegaard said "it is the God relationship that makes a man a man." Without God individuals melt into a faceless mass without differentiation. Quite consistently *The Humanist Manifesto II* advocates world government, and Karl Marx said back in 1844, "Communism is naturalized humanism."[11]

Onward and Upward

A second distinguishing mark of humanists is their optimistic belief in progress. Their dreams of the future have a utopian ring about them: "Humankind has the potential intelligence, good will and cooperative skill, which coupled with tolerance, understanding and peaceful negotiation will produce a world in which peace, prosperity, freedom and happiness will be widely shared."[12]

But this belief in what my student friend Ted called "the infinite perfectibility of human nature" can only be held by denying the tragic dimension of life. Blaise Pascal, the seventeenth-century philosopher and scientist who was also a profoundly committed Christian, wrote about "the grandeur and misery of man." Humanists, however, unwilling to come to terms with misery, see only grandeur. They resolutely refuse to face our nature as it really is.

Although unquestionably a great American, Thomas Jefferson was strongly influenced by the deists of his day who wanted a religion that fitted in better with their optimistic view of human nature than the Bible's emphasis on sin and the need for sacrifice and salvation. Jefferson decided to put together his own version of the Scriptures. The result—The Jefferson Bible—retained many of the ethical sections of the Bible. But it studiously left out any references to God's holiness, his forgiveness of sin or the cross of Christ as the sacrifice God provided for sin. These Jefferson perceived as crude concepts more fit for primitive times than capable of being accepted by rational men and women.

Inevitably his denial of human wrongdoing and of any need for a sacrifice for sin worked itself into the fabric of Jefferson's life. Jefferson had a beloved sister named Lucy. Lucy married a Dr. Charles Lewis, who was both a planter and a physician. The two moved westward into Kentucky with their two young sons, Lilburn and Isham. There they founded a plantation. After Lucy's death, Dr. Lewis moved back East and left the plantation in the hands of his two boys. On December 15, 1811, one of Lewis's slaves, named George, accidentally dropped and broke a pitcher that had been a prized possession of Lucy Jefferson Lewis. Furious at George's ineptitude, Lilburn and Isham decided to make an example of the clumsy slave. Before the eyes of all the other slaves, they proceeded to butcher him in the meathouse.

Fawn Brodie, one of the major biographers of Jefferson says, "One can only guess Jefferson's response to the tragedy."[13] More to the point, Robert Penn Warren in his epic poem *Brother to Dragons* explores the reasons Jefferson could not face up to the reality and horror of this event. To Warren the essential reason was that the sheer evil of the incident was too great a shock to the statesman's optimistic view of human nature.

It is never easy to face the horror of which human beings are capable. But our problem is compounded if we publicly espouse a view of human nature that denies such things can take place. If we lack a solution to any problem, we would prefer not to think about it. When J. Robert Oppenheimer, the scientist who had the most to do with developing the atom bomb, watched the first atomic bomb explode he recalled: "There floated through my mind a line from the Bhagavad-Gita: 'I am become death, the shatterer of worlds.' " In a tense meeting with President Truman after the war, Oppenheimer is recorded as having said: "Mr. President, I have blood on my hands." Truman, feeling very uncomfortable in Oppenheimer's presence, said to Dean Acheson: "Don't you bring that fellow around again. After all, all he did was make the bomb. I'm the guy who fired it off."

Beneath the surface optimism of the humanist you find a pessimist. This is why both existentialism with its denial of meaning and determinism with its denial of freedom are heirs of humanism. Bertrand Russell, one of the founders of modern humanism, had the honesty to face the despair inherent in his own philosophy:

> That Man is the product of causes which had no prevision of the end they were achieving; that his origin, his growth, his hopes and fears, his loves and his beliefs, are but the outcome of accidental collocations of atoms; that no fire, no heroism, no intensity of thought and feeling, can preserve an individual life beyond the grave; that all the labour of the ages, all the devotion, all the inspiration, all the noonday brightness of human genius, are destined to extinction in the vast death of the solar system, and that the whole temple of Man's achievement must inevitably be buried beneath the debris of a universe in ruins—all these things, if not quite beyond dispute, are yet so nearly certain, that no philosophy which rejects them can hope to stand. Only within the scaffolding of these truths, only on the firm foundation of unyielding despair, can the soul's habitation henceforth be safely built.[14]

Foundationless Morality

Humanism's broad tolerance in areas of sexual morality should not be taken as an indication of an indifference to moral questions. To the contrary, humanists are quick to extol virtues like compassion, honesty, justice, love and even humility. Many take their commitment to these virtues extremely seriously. However, what humanists lack is an objective reference point for right and wrong. Consequently, believing that all values are subjectively determined by the individual, when pressed, they are unable to give solid reasons for preferring these virtues to those based, for instance, on enlightened self-interest.

The burden of building an entire set of moral assumptions for oneself must weigh heavily on humanists. Since the possibilities are limitless and the guidelines from the past presumed to be often misleading, the responsibility is overwhelming. In 1967 Edmund Leach opened the Reith Lecture by saying: "Men have become like gods. Isn't it about time that we understood our divinity? Science offers us total mastery over our environment and over our destiny." Then he added, "Yet, instead of rejoicing we feel deeply afraid."[15] Being as gods, knowing good and evil has its downside, as the book of Genesis told us long ago.

Nevertheless, in the quest for moral principles humanists borrow unashamedly from other sources. In the *Humanist Manifesto II* the following values are lifted up as corporately shared by humanists: tolerance, humility, compassion, love for the outcast and honesty. At least two of those are directly lifted from the Bible, because the ancient Greeks had time neither for humility nor for love for the outcast. But although this should disturb humanists, it doesn't because in the end they are under no obligation to give a reason for choosing one set of values over another. Nor are they obliged to give a traditional meaning to those values they lift from the biblical source. They are quite free to define compassion for the outcast (read mentally retarded), for instance, as killing them.

When pressed for some sort of basis for morality, humanists usually cite nineteenth-century utilitarian John Stuart Mill, who said that we should always be guided by "the greatest good for the greatest number." A more modern way of saying the same thing is that people should be permitted to express themselves however they please as long as the fewest number are harmed. Choosing the area of sexual behavior to illustrate humanist moral principles, the *Manifesto* argues: "Short of harming others or compelling them to do likewise, individuals should be permitted to express their [sexual] proclivities and pursue their lifestyles as they desire." The results of this permissiveness are not always so attractive as the theory that advocates it. The contemporary reaction against the sexual revolution is coming, significantly, from those who, following just such a line, have found it a prescription for disease and tragically even death. Nature itself has sent our culture a resounding no to the endless pursuit of sexual pleasure; but who among the humanists is willing to admit that the original advice might have been faulty?

A Reason for Reason?

A fourth belief which humanists add to their faith in human nature, in progress and in the ability to construct a valid personal ethic without God is a deep faith in reason. Perhaps we should capitalize this as Reason! "Reason and intelligence are the most effective instruments that mankind possesses."[16] But there is of course a built-in contradiction between humanists' faith in Reason and their view of the individual whose "total personality is a function of the biological organism transacting in a social and cultural context," as the *Manifesto* puts it.

Humanists want to assume, on the one hand, that human beings are just biological organisms bouncing back and forth against their total environment and, on the other, that they possess something called Reason which can be an infallible guide to truth. But where does this Reason come from? And how do humanists know that Reason isn't just a vague longing that their own biological instincts have some ultimate meaning? G. K. Chesterton saw the need for something outside of our reason to guarantee its reliability. He said, "There can be no positive proof that we are not dreaming [when we reason], for the simple reason that no proof can be offered that might not be offered in a dream." Lacking an objective reference point beyond ourselves, we are finally imprisoned in our own subjectivity.

Descartes said, "I think, therefore I am." As a Christian I want to respond, "I am, therefore I think." Or, better: "God is; therefore I am; therefore I think." Without God, I am, as the humanists say, simply a biological organism transacting in a social and cultural context. With God, I am a human being with dignity and reason. When I use my reason, in some faint way I am mirroring the Mind that made me.

It is precisely on the level of evidence that humanism fails. While critical of Christianity in general, it makes no effort to come to terms with biblical claims about God or to interact with the realism of the Bible's view of humanity. It simply posits a different, and in the end naive, view of man. While it eschews the description of itself as a religion, it functions as just that—a deeply held conviction that human beings are essentially good, rational and destined for utopia once the restrictions and negatives of Christianity and its traditional ethics are thrown off. Capable of justifying the manipulation and even elimination of masses of human beings, it nevertheless passes itself off as the champion of compassion and humility. Seeing itself as the defender of Reason as over against superstition, it falls into the trap of elitism, for only those who believe themselves to be "rational" are in a position to decide what is best for the rest of humanity.

Humanism corresponds to Pharaoh's offer of abundance to the children of Jacob: "Come to me, and I will give you the best." But what appeared to be freedom was illusion, as the Hebrews painfully learned. Joseph was wise to keep in his mind the dream of "a better country" yet to come.

In an effort to carve out significance for human nature, humanists, using their own reason as a guide, end up singing with Swinburne "glory to man in the highest" and deifying man. But we wear our crown badly, and such undeserved exaltation makes us prey to grimmer assessments by the more realistic of the humanists and those who follow them. D. H. Lawrence, in _Women In Love,_ gives humanity this depressing epitaph: "There would be no absolute loss if every human being perished tomorrow. . . . Man is the mistake of creation."[17]

What Is Man?

On the great Paul Gauguin triptych in the Boston Museum, completed just before his death, the French postimpressionist painter asked three penetrating questions: "Where do we come from? What are we? Where are we going?" Our origin, our identity and our destiny are either unsolvable riddles, making a mockery of our fundamental desire to know why, or they drive us to deeper answers than humanists can give. Humanists hate the question "why?" As the posthumanist Nietzsche concluded: "Everything lacks meaning. . . . the goal is lacking; the answer is lacking to our 'why?' "[18]

Paul Gauguin needed to look no further than the Bible to have an answer to the question "What is man?" For while he contemplated the immensity of the night sky one evening, the psalmist asked:

When I look at thy heavens, the work of thy fingers,
   the moon and the stars which thou hast established;
what is man that thou art mindful of him,
   and the son of man that thou dost care for him? (Ps 8:3-4)

A few years ago my wife, Sandra, and I were hiking in the American Southwest. As we wandered in that geologist's paradise of canyons, outcroppings, buttes and mesas, our guide asked us more than once, "When you consider that you are looking at 800 million years of sedimentary rock, it makes you realize how insignificant you are, doesn't it?" Who would deny it? The truth of his observation is compounded when, using the geologists' time clock, one is reminded that if all time is compressed into twelve calendar months, the world had its origin on January 1, life appeared on July 22, mammals arrived on December 20, hominoids on December 28, and at 11:30 P.M. on December 31 human beings walked in.

True though this doubtless is, it has to be simply one part of the story. Because if the geologists have the whole story, then one must conclude as Reinhold Niebuhr put it that we are "little animals, living a precarious existence on a second-rate planet, attached to a second-rate sun."[19] We are left not with humanism, but with nihilism—the cry that all is absurdity and despair. But of course the optimism of humanism leads to the entrapment of nihilism.[20] But there is a way out for those willing to travel another way.

Refreshing Realism

By contrast with humanism's combination of extreme optimism and eventual pessimism, the Bible's view of human nature is refreshingly realistic. Preserved in a poetic form, yet doubtless with a historical core, the first three chapters of Genesis give us a view of human nature that we can recognize in ourselves.

In Genesis 1, which is surely more concerned with the "who" and "why" of creation than it is with the "how,"[21] we see that we are different from God, and God is other than we are. But we are also distinct from all the other animals. We are therefore neither divine beings nor dumb beasts. We are created "in God's image."[22] But only the context of this remarkable phrase can give us a clue as to its meaning.

The first clue comes immediately following the phrase "in our image," for God assigns us a rulership over the rest of his creation. We are to name the animals, thereby sharing in the task of giving these other creatures their unique identity.[23] We are to "subdue" the earth, a word far less rapacious than some environmentalists would claim, for other ancient Old Testament texts indicate that our care for our environment is to be that of a loving proprietor rather than a cruel master.[24]

A second clue to the meaning of "in God's image" is found in those passages in Genesis 1 which indicate that creation is the result of a decisive choice by God. Thus God says to himself, "Let us make . . ." This phrase would have been quite inconceivable to those who did not share the Hebrew mindset. Within the mythologies of the ancient Near East, "creation" had a kind of inevitability to it. It was either the result of a cosmic conflict between evil and good forces, or it was a direct emanation from the deity itself. In either case it was not the result of a clear choice made by a sovereign God.

But the biblical God decides in free will to create, and this unique ability to choose is passed on from God to those who are created in God's image. In Genesis 2:15-17 we see man and woman presented with the awesome choice of determining their own destiny. Between the alternatives of obedience and disobedience lies not only the choice to satisfy momentary appetite, but also more important the choice either to remain a dependent creature or to reach for the divinity which God reserved for himself.

The Bible tells us that as men and women we live in a world where our choices matter terribly. In light of the previous chapter, it is worth noting how different this is from the Buddhist view. In Herman Hesse's sensitive novel about the young Buddha, *Siddhartha,* good and evil are part of each other. Both are necessary. Because antithesis in the end doesn't exist, choices are not critical. What one must do is go with the flow, move with the river, accept the All and abdicate the painful responsibility to decide between one path of life over another.

A third clue as to the meaning of "in God's image" is to be found in the overall picture in Genesis 1—3 of a God who cares deeply about his creation, and especially about the man and the woman. He blesses them, provides for them, delights in them, is concerned about their loneliness, seeks communion with them, clothes them, and holds them accountable for their actions.[25] Moreover, as these passages show, God's desire to be in fellowship with people does not cease when they fall into disobedience and suddenly become his problem children. Quite the opposite. The man and the woman try to hide from God, but he comes to them, calls to them, listens to them and confronts them—all of which are powerful illustrations of his ongoing desire to maintain, or perhaps we should say rebuild, a relationship of extraordinary closeness.

To be made in God's image is to be capable of this sort of love relationship with God. Like all intimacy, as we have learned, it too is fraught with the potentiality of deep hurt and damage on both sides, but the possibility of love is still there. It is because God and his creatures were made to walk together in love that the decision of Adam and Eve to choose a path of their own was so disastrous for them and for us all. We live, then, with the tragic consequences of a choice that was originally not our own, and recapitulate that choice with our own willful rebellion against God. But we bear the image of our Maker nonetheless, and despite its present fragmentation this image can be made whole again.

It is thus in our ruling, our choosing and our loving that we are capable, while remaining a part of the organic, animal world, of having a special relationship which lifts us above it. Humanism, by seeking a way to elevate us from mere corporeality, robs us of the ability to find our true dignity in our relationship to God. It first turns us into gods, and then proceeds to smash the very idols it has made.

The Bible presents us with an understanding of humanity that corresponds with our own deepest intuitions. We know that we are significant, although limited. We know that we are moral, although flawed. And we know that we are individually responsible, although part of a wider human community. Moreover we know that whether we are a fetus in the womb, a handicapped newborn, a mental retardate or a senile old person, we are human, not because somebody has decided to confer personhood on us, but because in our relationship to God we discover who we are.

Reality Breaks Through

Although he was only one year behind me in college, John and I had never met until a relative suggested that he might want to talk to me about some questions that were troubling him. It was a lovely spring day in 1978 as this architect in his early forties and I sat out on the terrace and talked. For an hour and a half the questions literally flew. I was conscious then that exciting changes lay ahead for John. And indeed they did. What has unfolded since that day is a pilgrimage that in 1978 was still in its very earliest stages. I shall let him tell the story in his own words:

For twenty-five years I was a card-carrying member of the humanistic church, denying the existence of God, professing faith in man, and preaching the glories of the coming age, when men and women of both intellect and good will would govern a world flourishing under the application of scientific principles. Moreover, I was determined to be one of the leaders in that brave new world, as, I thought, my eight years of undergraduate and graduate training at Yale had prepared me to be. Unbeknownst to me, however, was the presence of an invisible hand in my life, with a will infinitely greater than mine and a plan for me very different from my own. Here is not the place to record all of its manifestations. One is relevant in this context. I read voraciously; and it seemed that, in every book which I read, I encountered a piece of evidence or an argument which undermined the humanistic religion which I had adopted. Slowly at first, and then more rapidly, my views regarding natural history, human history, human nature, and the nature of human knowledge began to change. Eventually I was forced to admit the reality of God. The incredible design of the universe required the hand of an equally awesome architect. How strange that such an idea took twenty-five years to penetrate the mind of a member of my profession.

Because it is one of man's most ancient records, my studies in natural and human histories took me into the Old Testament. I became well acquainted with its contents; and my estimation of its accuracy rose with each successive visit. One day it occurred to me to ask myself, if the Old Testament is reasonably reliable, is the New Testament equally so? Little did I foresee the consequences of that query.

One spring morning in 1980, alone in my study, I was reading in the Gospel of John when I experienced something so dramatic that my life can be divided into the time before and the time after. I changed. . . . In the process of what happened, I acknowledged before God that I had sinned and did repent of my sins, that Jesus Christ is his Son and my Lord, and that he was entitled to my service for the rest of my life, regardless of the costs. Three months later, I learned that, on that day, I had been "born again." . . . Until that day, I was blind to the spiritual world, but on that day, I glimpsed the Kingdom of God. It is real.

John found what millions have found—that humanism is bankrupt and incapable of answering the deepest quest of the heart. His story reminds me of a similar one three hundred years ago. Blaise Pascal, the seventeenth-century philosopher, scientist and mathematician found himself deeply concerned to combat the rationalists of his day. Mistakenly they thought that they could find truth through reason alone. Through a process whereby his eyes were opened to God in Jesus Christ, Pascal learned that real humanity could never be found apart from God, and that while reason is a great servant, it is a poor master. A loose translation of one of his better-known passages shows that he and John found much the same thing:

To look only at God breeds pride; to look only at ourselves breeds despair. But when we find Jesus Christ we find our true equilibrium, for there we find not only God, but ourselves as well.

One day, when Moses had grown up, he went out to his people and looked on their burdens; and he saw an Egyptian beating a Hebrew, one of his people. He looked this way and that, and seeing no one he killed the Egyptian and hid him in the sand. When he went out the next day, behold, two Hebrews were struggling together; and he said to the man that did the wrong, "Why do you strike your fellow?" He answered, "Who made you a prince and a judge over us? Do you mean to kill me as you killed the Egyptian?"

(EXODUS 2:11-14)

Having It Both Ways
The Relativist's Dilemma

ONDON: 1958

It was a beautiful Sunday afternoon—my very first in London as a
soon-to-matriculate graduate student at Oxford University. Since I had
plenty of time and there was no Hard Rock Cafe to serve as a mecca
for footloose Americans in those quieter days of the late 1950s, I
decided to wander over to Hyde Park. I had heard of "Speaker's
Corner" and was drawn by curiosity to see the speakers and observe
the crowd.

When I arrived I looked in amazement at the throng of people of
all sizes and ages squeezing around a dozen or more makeshift podiums. On the podiums—some made of orange crates, others of more
sophisticated materials—were a diverse group of advocates peddling
everything from Irish nationalism to something I remember identifying at the time as a bizarre form of Jewish apocalyptic.

After strolling about on the fringes of the crowds, I decided to pause
for a few moments to listen to a Salvation Army lassie. Her crowd

numbered roughly two hundred listeners, and it included a smattering of hecklers who chose to stand as close as they could to the podium so that their jibes could be heard by the rest of the people to everyone's amusement.

She was good, I thought. Simple, but clear and forceful. Resilient, too, given the barrage of humorous interruptions she had to withstand. Standing next to me was a sailor in his early twenties. He was listening attentively. Feeling an urge to discover whether his concentration was the result of spiritual hunger or mere curiosity, I turned to him and asked, "Hey, what do you think of what she's saying?"

He was surprised at this intrusion into his private thoughts and caught off guard. Perhaps my accent marked me as a recent arrival from across the Atlantic, or perhaps he was glad for a bit of human contact on a lonely weekend leave, but I found him very willing to talk to this complete stranger standing next to him. "Oh, I don't believe any of that stuff," he said.

I found his all-too-ready disclaimer unconvincing, so I decided to press on. "Why not? Don't you agree with what she's saying?" I can't remember the details of our conversation from that point on, but I noticed that within minutes we had gathered a little crowd around us who were eager to hear the debate between the American and the sailor. I recall both a wizened old lady and a young boy not more than fourteen among those who stayed with us.

As the two of us debated, a strange man with dark, penetrating eyes drew alongside us. He was wearing a blue duffel coat with a set of rolled-up blueprints coming out of one of the pockets. His shoulder-length black hair was neatly arranged in a page boy—a fact that drew my attention in those presixties days of short hair. A well-trimmed mustache and goatee completed the image of an artist or an architect. Out of the corner of my eye I caught a glimpse of him listening to us, and I was very surprised when, after a lengthy period of silence during which he seemed to take in all that was happening, he turned to the sailor and said, "Young man, you ought to listen and not to talk." With that he walked away.

Not long afterward, perhaps stunned by this unexpected rebuke from a man of such grooming and apparent perceptiveness, the sailor made an excuse to be off. Turning to the wizened old lady still at my side, I asked about the man in the duffel coat, "Who was that?"

As if she knew who he was, she said, "Oh, he's a very religious man, a very religious man."

By now my curiosity was thoroughly sparked, and with the fourteen-year-old boy trailing me, I went in search of this "very religious man." Finding him at the edge of another crowd, I walked up to him and said, "You look like an interesting man. What do you believe? What is your philosophy of life?" Somehow in those surroundings, with an assortment of Londoners listening to a smorgasbord of speakers, my question seemed entirely appropriate.

I found him willing enough to talk, but unwilling to give straight answers to my questions. Because he had previously indicated some sympathy with the Scriptures, but hadn't clearly identified with the position I was defending, I asked, "Are you a Jew?"

"It depends upon what you mean by a Jew," he answered.

I felt as if I was probing in the dark. "Do you believe in Armageddon?" I then asked, thinking that he might be a Jehovah's Witness. Their view of the end times predicts a literal and imminent fulfillment of the biblical prophecy of a final battle between God's forces and the devil's.

"Yes, I believe in Armageddon," he replied.

I pressed on, seeing what I thought was a bit of light at the end of the tunnel, "Do you believe that Armageddon is around the corner?"

He replied, "I believe that Armageddon is on the corner!"

But what did he mean? Once again, his answer seemed intentionally puzzling. Only later did I realize what he was implying—we were actually standing on a corner when he spoke.

But before I could figure all of that out, he fixed his eyes on me and asked, "Young man, do you know the crown of glory?"

I stumbled for an answer, drawing upon my fragmentary knowledge of the New Testament, "I think I remember something about it. Didn't St. Paul mention it somewhere—as a reward for a life well-lived?"

Then came a reply for which I was utterly unprepared, "I have seen the crown of glory in my Father's house."

I was so stunned that I repeated the words out loud, "You have seen the crown of glory in your Father's house?" It began to dawn on me that here before me was a man who was prepared, not only to claim unusual wisdom for himself, but also to claim to have a special relationship with God.

"You don't claim to be Jesus Christ?" I asked.

His reply was reminiscent of Jesus' answer to Pontius Pilate when asked "Are you the King of the Jews?"[1] Looking me straight in the eye, the man said, "You have said it."

I must have looked totally incredulous, for he then added, "I have the nailprints in my hands and feet."

"Let me see them," I asked.

He had gloves on. Shaking his head, he said, "Not for unbelieving eyes." He then proceeded to lecture me for two or three minutes for my hardness of heart and my unbelief, and then as unobtrusively as he had originally joined our little group, he simply walked away.

Particularly Scandalous

Naturally, I have thought about this incident many times. A man makes a claim to divinity and expects his hearers to believe implicitly. He permits neither questions nor reservations. I am expected simply to humble myself and believe.

Many in our modern era have comfortably accommodated themselves to the Eastern idea of a universal spirit or soul that can be found to a certain extent in everyone and in fuller measure in some. The modern mind is not particularly offended at the idea of a mystical Absolute in which all the constituent parts participate. This allows for great diversity on the human plane. As a society we have grown tolerant of gurus and mystics who claim to be indissolubly linked with the ultimate All. Many would side with Gandhi's assessment of the claims of Christ: "The soul of religions is one, but is encased in a multitude of forms. . . . Truth is the exclusive property of no single scripture. . . . I cannot ascribe exclusive divinity to Jesus. He is as divine as Krishna or Rama or Mahomed or Zoroaster."[2]

However, this Eastern idea that there is a universal soul is quite different from the claim that there is one God who is both personal and powerful and that a given historical person shares a privileged relationship with him. "I have seen the crown of glory in my Father's house" reeks with what theologians have called "the scandal of particularity"—one man claiming something that no others would. Against this the modern mind recoils.

The answer to why the modern mind rejects any notion of exclusivity lies in one of the subtle intellectual traps of the twentieth century—relativism. Relativism, the ethical partner to the cultural pluralism of modern society, stands resolutely opposed to any point of view claiming to be "the only way." Neither a thought-out philosophy nor a world view like monism or humanism, relativism is rather an attitude which people bring into the arena of moral judgments. It is, in fact, the hidden reservation which makes moral judgments so difficult to make.

Relativism says with bold clarity that there are no absolutes. It derives this conclusion from a prior premise that all moral principles have their source in the individual's own conscience. There are no such things as objective moral principles. This translates easily into the dogmatic insistence that no one can decide for another what is right or wrong. Only the individual, responding to a particular situation, can decide what for him or her is right or wrong.

Ostensibly, relativists make what appears to be an eminently tolerant statement. They would, of course, insist that certain values have great importance. With humanists they would want to put compassion, empathy, equality and nonviolence at the top of the list, along with tolerance. But whereas for humanists these values are taken to be self-evident, for relativists they must be only relatively valuable.

To be utterly consistent, relativists must agree that the logical implications of their position could be disastrous. If all values are merely the projections of individuals' wishes, can relativists, for instance, insist categorically that Hitler was wrong to murder six million Jews (and several million Christians, for that matter) but, on the other hand, that Albert Schweitzer was right to leave a promising musical career and establish a hospital in West Africa? Can relativists say with complete certainty that snake handlers in Tennessee are reprehensible religious fanatics, whereas Mother Teresa is a saint? Is it logically possible for relativists conclusively to condemn kamikaze drivers who, in the name of Allah, blow up buildings filled with innocent people, while commending the diplomats inside those buildings who are seeking just solutions in the Middle East?

Logically, of course, thoroughgoing relativists must agree that none of these extremes is objectively more or less moral than the others. They question the entire process by which we seek to make moral judgments. To them any ultimate confidence in one's own judgment is symptomatic of a fundamental flaw: the presumption that individuals have the right to decide what is moral for others. To relativists this is supreme arrogance.

According to relativists the supreme danger to a humane society is so-called true believers—people who are convinced with utter sincerity that in certain situations there is only one right way to act, or on certain issues only one right way to think. They are seen as confined to a limited viewpoint that if not checked or broadened may cause untold harm all in the name of religion or morality. True believers, as relativists see them, are the ones who, during the Crusades, descended on defenseless Middle Eastern Turkish towns in an attempt to impose medieval Christianity. Because of true believers innocent victims suffered at the hands of Inquisitors in the thirteenth to sixteenth centuries.[3] And the bombs that explode underneath busloads of innocent children in Northern Ireland are placed there by true believers.

Roots of Relativism

The roots of modern relativism are to be found in eighteenth-century philosophy and in twentieth-century science. Immanuel Kant (1724–1804), generally regarded as the philosophic bridge between rationalism and skepticism, believed along with his Enlightenment predecessors that reason was the only reliable guide to truth. Where his unique contribution lay was in the absolute separation of objective and subjective knowledge. Until Kant, it was widely assumed that all knowledge could fit together into one coherent (and, of course, reasonable) whole; but he stoutly maintained that there were two separate fields of knowledge, one of which yielded certain truth, while the other yielded only probable truth. In the scientific field where things could be objectively verified through empirical investigation, we could know things with absolute certainty. But in the realm of metaphysics, ethics, and religion there is no such certainty.

Although not a relativist (he believed, for instance, that reason could establish what he called the "categorical imperative"—moral guidelines that were universally valid because they could be universally applied),[4] Kant paved the way for relativism by claiming that religion and ethics must be removed from the realm of certain knowledge. This opened the door for the nineteenth-century subjectivists who saw all values (including faith and morals) as having their origin within the individual and as therefore having no objective validity in themselves.[5]

Kant's nearly absolute confidence in reason, marking him off as a true child of the eighteenth century, kept him from seeing the full impact of what he had done. If religion and morals are rationally unverifiable, then it follows that none of their statements could be taken as either absolutely true or absolutely false. It remained for nineteenth-century thinkers to extend the logic of Kant's thinking, jettison his precious reason, and build their systems on a totally subjective and irrational foundation. Although Kant would certainly have denounced relativism in its current form, his separation of knowledge into two irreconcilable fields paved the way for its emergence.

What Kant was to philosophy, Einstein was to science. Until Einstein's paper "On the Electrodynamics of Moving Bodies" was published in 1905, people believed in a stable, infinite universe where heavenly bodies moved in predictable patterns, where straight parallel lines would never meet, and where time was absolute. But Einstein's discoveries, and the proofs by which he verified them, upset this whole neat picture. According to Einstein the universe was not infinite but finite, though expanding. Straight, parallel lines do bend eventually; and time—on a clock, for instance, traveling at great speed—does actually slow down.

The foundations of Newtonian physics were shattered. Einstein's theory of relativity sent shock waves throughout the scientific world that understood its implications. Paul Johnson writes:

> It was grasped that absolute time and absolute length had been dethroned; that motion was curvilinear. All at once, nothing seemed certain in the movements of the spheres. "The world is out of joint," as Hamlet sadly observed. It was as though the spinning globe had been taken off its axis and cast adrift in a universe which no longer conformed to accustomed standards of measurement.[6]

It is doubtful that Einstein expected his theories to be applied as widely as they were. Although not a practicing Jew, he believed in God and was also a firm believer in absolute standards of right and wrong. He deeply lamented that his equation $E=MC^2$ opened the gate to the horror of nuclear warfare. But whether he liked it or not, a new idea had been sewn into the fabric of Western thought: everything is relative. Mistakenly, but perhaps inevitably, as Paul Johnson argues, relativity became one of the principal formative influences on the course of twentieth-century history. It cut society from its biblical moorings and cast it adrift to float wherever the winds would take it.[7]

In both philosophy and science, then, the stage was set for the triumph of relativism and its filtering down from the intellectuals and researchers to the masses. But it took the catastrophic effects of the First World War, the war that was called the "Great War" and the "war to end all wars," to usher it in as a foundational assumption of the modern age.

The Beast of Bethlehem

In Yeats's poem "The Second Coming," written in 1916, the anarchy that had been loosed on the land was as much moral and intellectual as political. To him it was clear that in the declining religious and moral standards of what was soon to become the "Roaring Twenties," Western society was adrift from its moorings. The conditions were ripe for some "rough beast . . . to slouch towards Bethlehem to be born."[8]

Yeats's new beast took the form of the social changes in the thirties and the forties that have altered the face of the world. Just as humanism with its boundless faith in humanity led to the creation of ideological utopias, so relativism, by creating a vacuum in which there are no absolutes, no values which transcend the cultural limitations in which they are found, helped produce the conditions within which actual dystopias would be born. Thus Lenin's Russia, Mussolini's Italy and Hitler's Germany arose in response to a need for an overarching vision and a comprehensive order for society.

Those who had once filled the ranks of totalitarian clergy would become totalitarian politicians. And, above all, the Will to Power would produce a new kind of messiah, uninhibited by any religious sanctions whatever and with an unappeasable appetite for controlling mankind. The end of the old order, with an unguided world adrift in a relativistic universe, was a summons to such gangster-statesmen to emerge. They were not slow to make their appearance.[9]

It is, in fact, demonstrable that the tyrannies of the twentieth century on both the right and the left are directly traceable to the intellectual and spiritual vacuum left by the coming of relativism. The goal of government is no longer to keep order, but rather to manipulate society toward ends which those in power deem socially desirable.

But is it fair to criticize relativism on the basis of certain extreme consequences? Most relativists would criticize these too, for to them all absolutes are anathema—political as well as religious. All they claim to want is a society where a variety of religious and moral positions are permitted, rather than a society where absolute power imposes a system of beliefs and behavior on all people.

They fear most of all the fanaticism of those who, without charity or self-awareness, seek to keep the faithful "in" and the apostate "out." Are there not abundant examples of how sincere religious conviction can become cultic and destructive? Is it not true that "men are excessively ruthless not as a rule out of avowed malice but from outraged righteousness?"[10]

But our sympathy for relativists confronted with the distortions of religious absolutists, must not blind us to the dangers of their fundamental premises. In a relativistic age the line between genuine conviction and fanaticism becomes blurred. Anyone slightly to the right of me is quickly branded "a fundamentalist" and conveniently lumped together with assorted despots like the Ayatollah Khomeini, Idi Amin and Sun Myung Moon, or with fanatics like the chanting Krishna devotees who pass out flowers at the airport.

Sincere Christians must be willing to admit that history is dotted with crusades, inquisitions, pogroms, even wars where religious certainty and the invocation of absolute virtue became the pretext, even if not the motive, for great harm. Before we presume to criticize the relativists we need to confess those parts of our heritage with shame. How else can we expect those who justifiably point out these blemishes on our record to listen to us further?

A New Meaning to Truth

Relativism, under closer scrutiny, can be shown to be vulnerable to a number of criticisms. Consider three corollaries of the relativist's assumption that truth is subjective:

Corollary 1: Truth emerges from consensus. Lacking any absolute, relativists look to the shared insights of individuals and communities for truth. Truth is arrived at by dialog, discussion and investigation. It is not arrived at by submission to a higher authority. Anything that smacks of preaching or the claim to have a corner on the truth is anathema. There are many different roads to the top of the mountain.

While those acclimatized to cultural relativism see this as eminently sensible, this view of truth contains a hidden and fatal flaw. The process of dialog, debate and discussion—which is quite valid in the quest for truth—necessarily involves the rejection of various ideas. Extreme suggestions, for instance, are automatically negated. And here, of course, is the hidden absolute. The making of any judgments between a Hitler and a Schweitzer or a Khomeini and a Mother Teresa assumes a hierarchy of values by which what is reasonable is separated from what is extreme. Deep within, relativists know that if one way is no better than another, then no way is good at all. Therefore, relativism quietly assumes it knows a better way.

Usually that better way is a midpoint between extremes. It is common to hear public figures, for instance, expressing personal disapproval of abortion, but saying that under no circumstance should abortions be denied those who want them. This is an attempt to have it both ways, arising from the corollary that truth emerges from consensus.

Corollary 2: Truth lies beyond antithesis. Relativists despise black-and-white thinking. In *Between Heaven and Hell,* Boston College philosophy professor Peter Kreeft imagines a conversation between Aldous Huxley, C. S. Lewis and John F. Kennedy, all three of whom, it happens, died on the same day, November 22, 1963. At one point Kennedy, the humanist, tries to resist the logic of Lewis, the Christian:

Kennedy: It's not clarity I can't stomach. It's black-and-white thinking.

Lewis: Isn't the second just a poetic way of saying the first? What do you mean by black-and-white thinking if not clarity?

Kennedy: It just isn't relevant to the world. The real world is gray. There are no absolutes, no black or white.

Lewis: You didn't answer my question, but I'll let that pass. Apparently you *do* mean "clarity" by "black-and-white thinking." And to say "there are no absolutes" sounds like a pretty absolute statement. Finally, I think I can convince you that there *are* some things that are black or white.

Kennedy: I challenge you. Name one.

Lewis: I'll name two.

Kennedy: Really?

Lewis: Yes. Black, and white.

Kennedy: That's just a trick.

Lewis: No, it isn't. It's like the statement, "There are no absolutes." It contradicts itself. It can't be true.[11]

Hating antithesis, relativists always look for truth somewhere beyond all opposites in a mystical combination of mutually exclusive ideas. Relativists see no need to be consistent. "Do I contradict myself?" asked Walt Whitman. "Very well then, I contradict myself. (I am large, I contain multitudes.)" Ralph Waldo Emerson claimed, "With consistency a great soul has simply nothing to do."

A mystical "Truth beyond truth and falsehood" ends up demolishing the idea of truth completely. For if it can be maintained that two mutually exclusive ideas are both true, then nothing is true. Friedrich Nietzsche once put it this way: "There are many eyes. Thus there are many truths. Hence there is no truth."

As a rebel from nineteenth-century traditional religion, Samuel Butler found that very few people really care about truth or have any confidence that truth ultimately matters. But not to care deeply about truth, he concluded, was a sign that whatever one professes to believe, one is an unbeliever in disguise.[12]

Corollary 3: Every deeply held conviction has a psychological basis. While opinions are all welcome, deeply held convictions in reality arise from needs deep within the psyches of those who hold them. Popularized by Freud, who discerned a basis for nearly everything in sex, this approach to absolutes claims to see through people's affirmations to the underlying motivations behind them.

Known as the "genetic fallacy," this point of view only confuses the issue. Even if it could be shown quite conclusively why a person does or does not hold a particular conviction, nothing has been said about its truth or falsehood. The result of this corollary is the effective destruction of truth itself. If I could "see through" everyone's deeply held convictions, I would be in the same position as if I could see through every object in the universe: I would see nothing.

Relativism has one further problem. Although widely assumed in theory, it is widely disregarded in practice. No one is really a relativist, practically speaking. Apply relativism to the real issues and then ask how many people really believe that other's views on racism are as true as theirs? On abortion? child pornography? atomic weapons? chemical warfare? gay rights? euthanasia? the legalization of hallucinatory drugs? support for covert though illegal government action?

Everyone has certain convictions about what they believe to be true or false. Few are willing to grant that what they believe and what those who disagree with them believe are both equally right. In the course of life we all make judgments about what is just and loving, what is good and bad. By doing so we assume that we are operating from a set of values that gives us a right to view others as wrong. While respect must be shown to people regardless of their views, none of us acts on the basis that those who profoundly disagree with us on crucial moral issues are just as right as we.

And relativists are no strangers to this practice. While avowing relativism when faced with true believers, at other times relativists proceed to make moral judgments on the basis of enlightened self-interest, which it is presumed will be for the benefit of society as well. All of which works reasonably well as long as one lives in a civilized society. But faced with tyranny, barbarism or injustice, it is relativists who either suddenly become fiercely absolutist or who opt out of responsibility and acquiesce in the status quo.

After teaching a course on the Holocaust at Harvard, Professor Robert M. Hunt discovered that the majority of his students considered the rise of Hitler inevitable, leaving no one responsible for the slaughter of six million Jews! He denounced such "no fault history" as unacceptable, but unacceptable or not, it must be seen as the logical consequence of the relativistic attitude of our age.[13]

The Strange Consensus

How should we approach relativists? Some Christians have tried by relying on general revelation. They begin by saying that because God has revealed himself generally through nature certain moral values are simply natural. These values are part of every human conscience, and no matter how different cultures are from one another we find a common thread running through them all pointing to a basic agreement on these natural values. In an incisive book, first published in 1947, C. S. Lewis calls traditional morality the Tao. Adducing evidence from cultures as varied as ancient Egyptian, old Norse, Babylonian, Hindu, Chinese, Jewish, Roman, "Redskin," Anglo-Saxon, Australian Aborigine and Christian, he shows that there has always been broad agreement on most fundamental moral values. Theorizing about the origins of this universal testimony, he writes:

It is by no means certain that there has ever . . . been more than one civilization in all history. It is at least arguable that every civilization we find has been derived from another civilization and, in the last resort, from a single centre—"carried" like an infectious disease or like the Apostolical succession.[14]

In the same vein sociologist Anthony Campolo points out that when Abraham Maslow tries to describe what he means by a "self-actualized human being," he draws freely on the values of Buddha, Lao-tse and the Koran, as well as the Old and New Testaments.[15] Moreover, Erich Fromm, writing as a secularist, builds his value system on an essentially Judeo-Christian foundation—but without God. Is there not broad agreement among the nations of the United Nations on a common ethical system, even though few, if any, actually live up to it? And have we not seen in chapter three how humanists cheerfully claim values like humility, love and compassion for their own system, even if they have no final reason for choosing them over their opposites?

A Shocking Revelation

Quite a different response to the problem of relativism arises from what theologians call special revelation—that unique witness in history, stretching through the centuries, to the self-disclosure of one infinite and personal God. We find this in the Bible.

From the relativist's perspective, some account must be given for the fact that somewhere in the region of ancient Mesopotamia in the Middle Bronze Age (20th-19th centuries B.C.), a man by the name of Abraham got the idea that there was only one God. The historicity of Abraham, though to my mind well established, is irrelevant here. The fact that someone made this unique claim is undeniable in view of subsequent events. It is easy for the staggering nature of this "discovery" to escape us until we remember that Abraham's culture was rich in religious diversity. A plurality of gods coexisted in the consciousness of the people and vied with each other for people's attention. But Abraham parted company with his family and compatriots and set out on a journey across the Fertile Crescent for only one ostensible reason: the one and only God told him to go.

Centuries later, most likely in the thirteenth century B.C., a man named Moses, standing in a direct line of witness stretching back to Abraham, had a revelation somewhere on the Sinai Peninsula while watching a bush burn without its being consumed. Startled by the sight, he heard a voice telling him that the same God whom Abraham had encountered is a holy God, an eternally existing God, and a God with a special mission for him.

Over the centuries that followed, history records a stream of men with names that Bible readers recognize—Amos, Hosea, Isaiah, Jeremiah, Ezekiel, Daniel—all proclaiming the will and purpose of this God. In great detail and with striking unanimity, given the long time span over which they wrote, they describe this God and speak of his desire to form a people who would be the means of passing this revelation on to the rest of the world.

Then after hundreds of years comes what C. S. Lewis called "the real shock." Among these Jews there suddenly turns up a man who goes about talking as if he was God. He says he has always existed. He says he is coming to judge the world at the end of time. He claims to have the authority to forgive sins.

Remember, this man arose within a people who had stoutly maintained for some sixteen to twenty centuries that there was only one God and that he had revealed himself to them. And so the claim of this man Jesus to be this revelation in person had to be taken seriously. History records that in fact it was taken with deadly seriousness by his contemporaries. Some of them killed him for it, while others gave up their lives because of it.

If it can be said, as philosopher Will Durant has said, "in all of Western civilization, the person who stands out above all others is Christ. He undoubtedly was the most permanent influence on our thoughts."[16] And if, as it has been estimated nearly 2,000 years later, now more than 950 million people claim some allegiance to Christ, then what claim to intellectual honesty can we possibly have without ourselves coming to terms with him?

Facing Jesus Christ

On a dusty Galilean road, surrounded by his closest friends one day, Jesus suddenly asked: "Who do men say that the Son of man is?" It was a direct challenge to them. Choose sides! They replied: "Some say John the Baptist, others say Elijah, and others Jeremiah or one of the prophets." But Jesus, wanting them to make up their minds, then asked: "But who do you say that I am?" It was Peter who grasped the nettle and replied, "You are the Christ, the Son of the living God."[17]

But what are our options today? They are not fundamentally different from those I faced when I was confronted in 1958 with a "very religious man" in Hyde Park. I had exactly three. Either he was deluded, or he was a deceiver, or he was the Messiah he claimed to be.

It is often argued that there is a fourth possibility in regard to Jesus, and we should consider that here before we look at the three I have mentioned. Popularized in 1977 by six British theologians in a book entitled *The Myth of God Incarnate,* this hypothesis argues that while Jesus, the carpenter rabbi of Nazareth, saw himself as the Messiah of Israel, he never intended his followers to see him as God in the flesh. Nor did his Apostles see him as such. Rather it is the pious devotion of later disciples, whose simple faith embellished the sayings and stories of Jesus into their present form, to which we must credit the church's eventual faith in his divinity.

These theologians point out, quite rightly, that the idea of a human/divine Messiah would have been foreign to the monotheistic mindset of first-century Jews. However, they conclude, quite wrongly, that such an idea would then have had to come from the Hellenistic world where dying and rising gods were part of the common mythological world view.

Their efforts at tracing the belief in the full divinity of Jesus to cultural influences blind them to the fact that while Hellenistic culture, according to J. G. Frazer's *Adonis, Attis, and Osiris,* was filled with stories of dying and rising gods, not one of these stories made any identification of these gods with historical personages. Thus we see what was utterly unique about the Gospel writings both for the Greek as well as the Jewish culture of the day; namely, the bringing together of these two elements: a historical person, whom many people knew, and the eternal "myth" of a god who descends, dies and rises again.

This should give us pause before attempting to find a cultural source for that utterly unique feature found in all the New Testament writers; namely, that Jesus was very much a human being—like you and me—yet at the same time possessed by extraordinary powers over disease, the demonic and death—unlike you and me.

What is really striking about the stories about Jesus that the Gospel writers handed down to us is their restraint. Had they wanted to embellish an originally simple tale, or had they wanted to feed the faith of the superstitious masses of first-and second-century believers, how could they have resisted giving us stories of stones turned into bread, buildings demolished and reconstructed in an instant, and discarded crutches piled at the entrace of the empty tomb? No, Jesus refused to attempt miracles in certain places simply because he did not want to feed that kind of faith. Rather the miracles of Jesus we have recorded are those that carry a specific message. It is a message, not primarily of his divinity, but rather of his saving mission. They are "signs" of the downfall of evil, the victory of life over death, the replacing of judgment with mercy, and the power of love that conquers fear. As such they dovetail remarkably with his claims and his character into a total witness which confronts the honest seeker today with the need for response just as it did while he roamed Judea. For the disciples divinity was an identity they couldn't help but confer on Jesus once the meaning of his message was grasped, and once they were confronted with the evidence for his resurrection from the dead.

Placing this fourth option to one side, we now consider the other three. We must admit that it is theoretically possible that Jesus was deluded as to his true identity. People who believe themselves to be superhuman are found in mental institutions around the world. At one point early in his ministry the frenzy surrounding Jesus and the energy coming from him were so troubling to onlookers that the rumor began to be circulated: "He is beside himself."[18] Momentarily, even his family was concerned. But can we so easily dismiss Jesus? I found that in 1958 I had no difficulty dismissing that "very religious man" as deluded. In fact, I wasn't in the least surprised when the *London Times* soon reported that Scotland Yard was on the lookout for a man who neatly fitted his description. The wanted man had last been seen chiseling things suspiciously into the ancient stones at Stonehenge!

History has never been comfortable with this judgment on the person of Jesus. Very few of his contemporaries saw him as unstable. The people who loved him ranged from hard-bitten tax collectors to rough fishermen. Men, women and children flocked to him. A lunatic might claim, as Jesus did, that he was "the way, and the truth, and the life,"[19] but it is highly doubtful that he would get people as different as the emotional Mary Magdalene and the shrewd tax collector Zacchaeus to believe him. In part because of his influence on the people and also because of the total clarity of his message, his enemies never seriously sustained the thought that he was deluded.

We have to answer disturbing questions such as: Where else in history do you find a man who had such an ability to speak to others of the evil in their hearts and yet make no confession of evil in his own? Where do you find a person so at ease with notorious sinners, yet able to ask his closest friends "Which of you can convict me of sin?" and get silence for an answer? Where has there been a man so totally humble who, without blushing, could allow people to fall at his feet and worship him? Despite the song put into Jesus' mouth by the writers of *Jesus Christ Superstar* in which he asks "Am I really who you say I am?" and despite Nikos Kazantzakis's efforts in his novel *The Last Temptation of Christ* to present us with a Jesus torn between the pull of the spirit and the lusts of the flesh, there is absolutely no evidence to be gained from a plain reading of the four Gospels that he was ever confused or uncertain or deranged—especially about his identity as the Anointed One of God.

But then, secondly, could he have been intentionally deceiving others? Might he not have hoped that by forcing the issue of Messiah's arrival he could have hastened in some way the coming of the Kingdom? According to this hypothesis, he could have arranged the details of his life to fit in with Old Testament prophecies foretelling that the Messiah-king would enter Jerusalem humbly on a donkey and then get himself crucified exactly as David and Isaiah foretold.[20] But again, is this likely given the character of the man?

There was a purity and a truth about him which lent amazing authority to whatever he said.[21] He was transparent to the point of saying "I am humble and meek," and no one questioned it. In his presence few people could hide the truth about themselves, and many found the freedom to be radically honest about things long covered up.[22] Also, the God whom he repeatedly called Father in a most intimate way was One who saw into people's deepest thoughts and demanded utter integrity in people's words, motives and actions.[23] It is recorded that even his enemies were prepared to confess that he spoke and taught truthfully.[24]

Speaking of the unique character of Jesus when compared to the culture in which he lived, Boris Pasternak wrote:

> Rome was a flea market of borrowed gods and conquered peoples, a bargain basement on two floors, earth and heaven, a mass of filth convoluted in a triple knot as in an intestinal obstruction. . . . Eyes sunk in fat, sodomy, double chins, illiterate emperors, fish fed on the flesh of learned slaves. . . . All wretched. And then, into this tasteless heap of gold and marble . . . He came. Light—and clothed in an aura. Emphatically human, deliberately provincial, Galilean. . . . At that moment gods and nations ceased to be and Man came into being.[25]

The third option is to confess Christ as the Lord he claimed to be. A full knowledge of all that this implies in terms of his divinity is really not needed at this point—just a humble acknowledgment that he is God. Whenever there is a willingness to bow one's mind before him as having the final and absolute word, the light dawns.

Why do people hesitate to take this step? If Jesus was neither deceived nor a deceiver, he must have been who he claimed to be. But how can we be sure? No learned authority can certify to us that Jesus really was the Son of God. While many wish for just such certification, he does not permit us to rely on anyone else's judgment. We are left with the ultimate witness: the force of his own character and the manifest truth of his teaching.

The centuries record how Jesus' words have passed into laws, into poetry, into hymns, into literature and into theology. But they have never passed away. "Heaven and earth will pass away," said Jesus, "but my words will not pass away."[26] It was the Greeks, not the Hebrews, who believed that you could separate a person's words or thoughts from their character, but for those who encountered Jesus Christ the two were inextricably intertwined. To meet him was to be captivated by him. It was to discover not just an authority before which to bow, but a living Word which gave life an entirely new meaning. How else do we account for how Peter was transformed from a coward into a leader, and Thomas from a doubter into a worshiper, and Zacchaeus from a thief into a philanthropist, and Mary Magdalene from a prostitute or at the least a very sick woman into a saint, and Paul from a pharisaical persecutor into the apostle to the Gentiles?

A Cosmic Question Mark?

Try to imagine a world in which people's search for Truth is never satisfied. Would you not conclude that everything is absurd? Samuel Beckett found neither certainty nor meaning. Life is perpetually waiting for a Godot who is never coming. Life remains a guessing game with no answers. A song in the musical *Hair* asks: "Is there an answer? Tell me why; tell me why; tell me why." Men and women down the centuries have longed for answers. They have hungered to know the basic meaning of life. They have sought God. What a cruel joke it would be if the creator of such a world had left no way for them to know!

The one person a relativist cannot relativize is Jesus Christ. Dividing history into B.C. and A.D., he still presents us with a question that no honest thinking person can escape: "Who do you say that I am?"[27]

In his autobiography, British journalist and literary critic Malcolm Muggeridge put his own struggle to come to terms with the towering figure of Jesus this way:

I knew from a very early age—how I cannot tell—that the New Testament contained the key to how to live. I somehow knew it to be our only light in a dark world. Not just in my father's sense that Jesus himself was a good man, and his moral precepts greatly to be admired. . . . [I understood that] Jesus could not be turned into just a [great man] without diminishing him to the point that Christianity became too trivial to be taken seriously. He was God or he was nothing.[28]

At midnight the LORD smote all the first-born in the land of Egypt, from the first-born of Pharaoh who sat on his throne to the first-born of the captive who was in the dungeon, and all the first-born of the cattle. And Pharaoh rose up in the night, he, and all his servants, and all the Egyptians; and there was a great cry in Egypt, for there was not a house where one was not dead. And he summoned Moses and Aaron by night, and said, "Rise up, go forth from among my people, both you and the people of Israel; and go, serve the LORD, as you have said. Take your flocks and your herds, as you have said, and be gone; and bless me also!"

And the Egyptians were urgent with the people, to send them out of the land in haste; for they said, "We are all dead men."

(EXODUS 12:29-33)

A Cry in the Night
The Narcissist's Fear

THE CURRENT USE OF THE WORD NARCISSISTIC *TO DE-*
scribe a cultural trend in the affluent West has a pedigree worth
noting. An ancient Greek myth about Narcissus had been told and
retold for centuries, but the version with which we are most familiar
is that of the Roman poet Ovid. As he explained it, a handsome young
man named Narcissus was told that he would enjoy a long life as long
as he never gazed at an image of himself. But as fate would have it,
one day he happened to look down into a pool of water and there
he saw for the first time an image of himself. Unfortunately for him,
it was love at first sight! He became so infatuated, in fact, that he could
not respond to the attempts of a nymph named Echo to win his love.
His punishment for this infraction began when, after repeated attempts to touch and kiss his reflection, the goddess Retribution saw
to it that he died. Then, in the underworld, he was appropriately
condemned to an eternity of frustrated infatuation with his own image
as he saw it reflected in the River Styx.

In the nineteenth century Sigmund Freud seized on this myth as a way of illustrating a psychological disorder that occurs when a person fails to direct his or her sexual energy first toward the parent and then, in maturity, toward another person; but rather turns that sexual energy in on himself or herself and becomes incapable of establishing a genuine sexual relationship with another.

By the 1970s narcissism was coming to be used in a frame of reference wider than either its mythic or Freudian antecedents. For the first time people were described as "clinically" narcissistic. Psychiatrists began observing that people were no longer coming in large numbers complaining of feelings of guilt. Rather they were coming complaining of a sense of inner emptiness, of unsatisfied relationships, of an incapacity to love and of feelings of meaninglessness. It had become rare for people to come with feelings of being uptight, unable to express emotions and bottled up. Rather they were coming with the opposite problem: an inability to control their emotions, to keep their passions in proper balance, and to gain any satisfaction from the relationships in which they were involved.

This broadening of Freud's use of the term led to a need for a new set of diagnostic criteria for therapists. In the 1978 draft of a 1980 article on narcissistic personality disorders in the American Psychiatric Association's _Manual,_ a new list of criteria were spelled out. They included a "grandiose sense of self-importance or uniqueness; focusing on how special one's problems are; preoccupation with fantasies of unlimited success, power, brilliance, beauty, or ideal love; exhibitionistic need for constant attention and admiration; feelings of rage, inferiority, or emptiness in response to criticism or defeat; lack of empathy; sense of entitlement without assuming reciprocal responsibilities; tendency to take advantage of others and disregard their personal integrity."[1]

Stuck on Oneself

In everyday language, clinically ill narcissists see the world as a mirror. Coming into a room full of people, they do not see other people with needs, problems and life experiences to learn from. What they see is an audience—people to impress, to be admired by and from whom to gain a measure of self-esteem. Because of their underlying insecurity, narcissists will tend to gravitate to those who radiate celebrity and charisma or power and influence. These are the people who must be impressed and charmed and by whom it is essential to be admired. If personal values must be bent in the process, so be it. They are totally subservient to this need. It will be expected that relationships will become manipulative and will be short-lived because narcissists' self-absorption prevents them from being truly faithful despite an intense hunger for something lasting and deep.

Paul Vitz calls narcissism "the most rapidly increasing clinical syndrome and . . . lively theoretical issue in psychotherapy today."[2] Spilling beyond the confines of those considered clinically ill, narcissism is no longer just a personality disorder discernible to the psychiatrist. It is a cultural phenomenon that permeates our entire society. The most comprehensive book describing the eighties from this perspective is entitled *The Culture of Narcissism—American Life in an Age of Diminishing Expectations* by Christopher Lasch, a University of Rochester historian. Since the publication of his book, a spate of books and articles have appeared—all characterizing our culture as narcissistic. The eighties were "the *me* decade."

Lasch makes the interesting point that if we want to understand a culture we should look at its sicker members. Emotional illnesses, he claims, are culturally induced and reinforced. Therefore, when you understand the neuroses prevalent at any given time, you then have insights into the problems which in milder forms plague the culture as a whole.

Cracks in the Mirror

Listing all these problems is beyond the scope of this chapter, but perhaps a few will illustrate my point. Ours is first of all a culture that

114 ————————————————————————————— DISARMING THE SECULAR GODS

is hostile to authority of all kinds. Personal rights become pitted against rightly constituted authorities so that the only final authority is the self. Because the modern world tells us that we are autonomous, that there is no God who created us, who sustains us, who will one day judge us, and to whom we owe respect and allegiance, we are obliged to no one but ourselves. There are no others to whom we belong or whose interests we should put before our own.

Second, our culture has become fearful of dependence. Women fear dependence on men; men fear deep attachment to women. We celebrate the bionic man and the bionic woman. These media creatures are full of experiences of all kinds—especially sexual ones—but they are empty shells of people incapable of building lasting relationships. Parents fear children who seem too dependent on them. Counselors fear dependent patients, and teachers fear dependent pupils.

Third, our culture manifests great preoccupation with the self. *Self-actualization, self-reliance, self-esteem, self-love, self-fulfillment* have become regular household words. Paul Vitz recalls the following advertising copy from *Psychology Today:*

> I love me. I am not conceited. I'm just a good friend to myself. And I like to do whatever makes me feel good. We live by a certain philosophy: we try to make our dreams come true today, instead of waiting for tomorrow. But before you can do good things for yourself, you have to know yourself. . . . You need self-knowledge before you can have self-satisfaction. Think about it.[3]

We can see signs of this narcissistic concentration on the self in the advertising that urges impulse gratification and in professional athletics where celebrities and superstars, their bodies streamlined by performance-enhancing drugs, have replaced real achievers. The same trend is apparent in religion, which has to so many become merely a thinly disguised therapy ("I feel good when I go to church; I find inner peace" and so forth), and in education, where schools are more concerned to socialize pupils so that they can adjust to each other than they are with imparting information. It's not that all of this is wrong. There is a healthy affirmation of the self rooted in our being created in the image of God. Personal expression has a long and honorable history in Christianity—especially in the arts. But it can and often does go too far. In a *New Yorker* cartoon, a first-grade teacher sits cross-legged on the floor with her pupils around her in a circle. She is looking at a puzzled little boy and saying, "Tell us, William, if you can, how you feel about first grade."

Rakes Progress

It's a long road from Ovid's myth through Freud's sexual fixation to "clinical narcissism" and finally to a narcissistic culture. But we can't seem to escape the shadow of this attractive young man.

There once was a lad named Narcissus
Who thought himself very delicious.
So he stared like a fool
At his face in a pool,
And his folly today is still with us.

To modern-day narcissists, or the products of our narcissistic culture, an encounter with Christianity elicits a deep gut-level objection. Their basic problem is not doctrinal nor is it intellectual. Their real struggle is with the idea of dependence. Anything which causes one to surrender one's autonomy is totally unacceptable. And, of course, Christianity at its most basic level cannot authentically be presented apart from dependence. The Bible depicts us as dependent on God as our creator and sustainer. We are called to depend on Jesus Christ as savior, and we must stand before him as judge. We rely on the Spirit's empowering to live the Christian life. The most radical statement of this dependence is found in Jesus' word to the disciples: "Apart from me you can do nothing."[4]

To Jesus the self was not paradise. Nor would releasing it, expressing it, fulfilling it, or actualizing it ever bring in the kingdom of God. On the contrary, the self is our problem. Only those who lose their selves can find them. Only those who prefer others before themselves can serve with honor in his fellowship. Only those willing to be last in this world's terms are first in his. Only those who die to their self-centered selves know in an ongoing way the life he came to bring.[5]

To the narcissist Christianity requires the loss of the most precious thing one has: the self. All the altruistic and selfless sentiments of the New Testament are inherently distasteful. Russian-born U.S. author Ayn Rand sees them as the very antithesis of those qualities necessary for achievement. To Rand the modern hero is the strong self-made person who by egoism and genius triumphs over timid traditionalism and social conformity.[6] Narcissists have on their side, at least in terms of the centrality of the self, weighty modern apologists like John Dewey, who in a kind of Ptolemaic reaction to the Copernican Revolution placed man once again squarely at the center of things, and like Abraham Maslow, who proclaimed self-actualization as the ultimate value in his scale of human needs.[7]

In the 1987 Warner Brothers film _The Mission_, Mendoza (Robert De Niro) converts to Christianity from capturing seventeenth-century South American Indians for slaves. He makes a convincing convert, but in the end refuses to follow his mentor, Father Gabriel (Jeremy Irons), in his suicidal pacifism when confronted by Portuguese mercenaries. Mendoza takes up arms. The viewer is left to decide whether his response is out of weakness or heroism. But in the context of twentieth-century culture those unpersuaded by Father Gabriel's martyr spirit will doubtless see Mendoza as a man of action, someone whose self has not been fully crucified by Christian piety.

If the Shoe Fits

At times the loss of the self has been presented under the guise of Christian teaching in a destructive way. Watchman Nee, a saintly Chinese preacher and teacher, widely respected in the Christian world, identified the soul with the self-life and wrote extensively about how, in the crucifixion of the soul with Christ, the believer loses all right to act independently of God:

> You lose that power to act when you come to know the Lord. The Lord cuts it off and you find you can no longer act on your own initiative. You have to live by the life of Another; you have to draw everything from Him.[8]

It is, of course, a half-truth and dangerous. I have met some Christians, alive with religious fervor, who seem to have lost their personalities. At the lunatic fringes of the Christian movement are cults which appear to abound with devotees whose plastic smiles eclipse their true humanity. One is reminded of Dostoevsky's caricature of the medieval church as having taken away people's freedom and replaced it with "miracle, mystery and authority."[9] There are some highly structured Christian fellowships today where the ministry of "shepherding" becomes a euphemism for rigid control of young believers by their spiritual elders.

Within evangelical Christianity are elements that foster a ghetto mentality. The self is not permitted healthy expression because of a constant fear of contamination by the world. While at the liberal end of the theological spectrum, although much may be made of the individual's conscience, the thrust of the message preached is essentially a call to collective social improvement, often to the neglect of personal spiritual transformation. In both cases there is an unhealthy departure from the kind of self-concern which is firmly rooted in the teaching of Jesus and Paul. For Jesus taught that no one can love others well if they do not love themselves, and Paul wrote that "no man ever hates his own flesh, but nourishes and cherishes it."[10]

Do not construe what I have said as even partial justification for narcissism. Narcissism is not a thought-out view of the world with merits that must be given due weight alongside the merits of other systems. It is, rather, a flight from responsible decision making and in its worst forms an implosion of the self in upon itself that renders impossible what normal people call maturity.

Psychologist Dan Kiley links narcissism with the relentless pursuit of perfection by people whose insecurities have become a hostile army within themselves. Life is an obsessive effort to respond to the critical voice within, with the result that victims never grow up into responsible adulthood. They may become locked in what Kiley calls the Peter Pan Syndrome. Peter Pan, who overlooked others like Wendy, who tried to be helpful, needed constantly to hear stories about himself to reinforce his zeal for perfection. Similarly, the modern narcissist staves off loneliness and fear by compulsive perfectionism. Rather than facing his insecurities, "he compensates for his gross imperfections by remaining in his mirrored room, seeing what he wants to."[11]

Narcissism is self-destructive. If I concentrate on myself, I eventually destroy myself. We were made for community and for relationships. That is why *Swiss Family Robinson* is inherently more believable than *Robinson Crusoe*. We need the love of others to survive. An experiment in the sixteenth century proved this without a doubt. King Frederick II (1712-1786) arranged for several babies to be segregated at birth. They were neither talked to nor cuddled, but nurses saw to it that all their physical needs were met. His intention was to seek to discover what the true language of humanity was. He eventually found it out, though it was tragic for the little children. All of the babies used in the experiment died. They literally died from a lack of love.

The point is that we are social animals, and everything that isolates, separates and makes meaningful relationships impossible is very destructive to the self. Studies show that people who look to others to feed their own self-esteem may appear to have a very high degree of self-love. But what appears to be self-love is soon followed by self-hate, and with it a general mood of meaninglessness.[12]

Beyond being self-destructive, narcissism is unrealistic. An approach to life which does not take into account the warp in human nature is bound to be unrealistically utopian. In *Who Will Deliver Us?* Paul Zahl quotes noted columnist Ellen Goodman who describes the model woman of today:

She gets up at six-thirty in the morning and jogs five miles. At seven-thirty she cooks a totally nourishing breakfast for her husband and two beautiful children. By eight-thirty the children have left for school, her husband to his office, and she is on the way to her incredibly demanding job: she is advertising director for a major firm. All day long she attends meetings, makes important decisions. When she finally arrives home, it is quite late because she had to attend a board meeting for a community-service organization of which she is chairman. But she does not get home too late to fix her children a totally nourishing supper. She helps both of them with their homework, and has meaningful good-nights with each. Yet she still has time to plug in the Cuisinart to prepare a gourmet, candlelit supper for herself and her husband. As the day comes to an end, the Model Woman has a totally fulfilling yet deeply honest sexual relationship with her admirably sensitive husband.[13]

But reality forces us to ask our Model Woman (or her deeply sensitive husband for that matter): What about stress? What about depression? What about anger? Frustration? What about all the negative aspects of the self with which most of us contend daily? Can you show me a man or a woman who doesn't struggle with these? By contrast, the realism of the Bible gives us a no-nonsense picture of human nature: "The heart is deceitful above all things, and desperately corrupt; who can understand it?"[14]

Inescapably Yours, Sin

John Newton, the eighteenth-century slave trader-turned-clergyman, who composed "Amazing Grace," once wrote a simple verse describing the attitude of a person who had come to see himself in an entirely new light while pondering the enormous contrast between his own character and God's. Walking along the seashore Newton had these thoughts:

In ev'ry object here I see
Something, O Lord, that leads to thee;

Firm as the rocks thy promise stands,
Thy mercies countless as the sands,
Thy love a sea immensely wide,
Thy grace an ever-flowing tide.

In ev'ry object here I see
Something, my heart, that points at thee:
Hard as the rocks that bound the strand,
Unfruitful as the barren sand,
Deep and deceitful as the ocean,
And, like the tides, in constant motion.[15]

Without the slightest sense of what the Bible calls sin, modern narcissists look for someone or something to blame for the evil and corruption which leaves its indelible print on all of society. If Adam blamed Eve and Eve blamed the serpent, then it is only to be expected that people today will find someone other than themselves on whom to pin the blame. A convenient place to lay the blame, as Pharaoh found in ancient Egypt, Nero in first-century Rome, Hitler in modern Europe and persecutors throughout the ages is with those whose faith in God marks them off as separate and distinct. No wonder Ezra Pound found fascism so attractive, for in his conviction that the phallus not the cross points the way to heaven, he had concluded that "all established churches are an outrage" and Christianity is a "bastard faith devised for the purpose of making good Roman citizens or slaves."[16]

In a more humorous vein, modern fathers I fear will take little comfort from a cartoon that appeared in *Punch* showing two nice little girls playing together. One of them asks the other, "Do you believe in the devil?" The other replies, "Of course not, silly; it's like Santa Claus; it's only Daddy."[17] Psychiatrists have often turned others into the scapegoats of our own problems. In a "psychiatric folk song" which lampooned this viewpoint, Anna Russell wrote:

At three I had a feeling of
Ambivalence toward my brothers,
And so it follows naturally
I poisoned all my lovers.
But now I'm happy; I have learned
The lesson this has taught;
That everything I do that's wrong
Is someone else's fault.[18]

Until he became a Christian, Aleksandr Solzhenitsyn thought evil was fundamentally external to humanity. But then he wrote: "Gradually it was disclosed to me that the line separating good and evil passes not through states, nor between classes, nor between political parties either—but right through every human heart." Today, even the psychiatric community is coming to see that a sense of sin is necessary. In *Whatever Became of Sin?* Karl Menninger argued that the doctrine of sin brings a sense of responsibility for our behavior and therefore the possibility of real reformation—not the helpless attitude of the narcissist who is consumed with feelings of meaninglessness.

To these two weaknesses, I believe we must add a third: narcissism is superficial. Narcissism does not exist in cultures where people have to do an honest day's work to make ends meet. It is an approach to life that lives like a parasite off economic prosperity and affluence. As Brian Walsh, coauthor of *The Transforming Vision: Shaping a Christian World View,* puts it: "Homo economicus is the necessary foundation for modern homo narcissus." You simply must have plenty of time to fulfill, to actualize, to satisfy and to express yourself—to say nothing of lots of cash to spare. If bored, you can always go shopping in one of the new malls which have grown like soft cancers on the edges of our cities. Malls have become places of community for the lonely. The advertising moguls know our weakness for impulse gratification. Lasch says:

Advertising upholds consumption as the answer to the age-old discontents of loneliness, sickness, weariness, lack of sexual satisfaction. . . . Is your job boring and meaningless? Does it leave you with feelings of futility and fatigue? Is your life empty? Consumption promises to fill the aching void; hence the attempt to surround commodities with an aura of romance, with allusions to exotic places and vivid experiences, and with images of female breasts from which all blessings flow.[19]

But who is really fooled? At least on an intellectual level most people realize that these needs cannot be satisfied in such superficial ways. Today's advertising only creates new forms of discontent. As I have heard it said: there is only one thing to give the person who has everything—your deepest sympathy.

We are forced to the conclusion that even in its milder, more socially acceptable forms, narcissism fails to deliver what it promises. It promises fulfillment and delivers emptiness; it promises relationship and delivers loneliness; it promises joy and delivers depression. One person put the contrast between narcissism and Christianity this way: "Christianity starts with suffering and ends with joy. Narcissism starts with optimism, but ends with pessimism."

The Paradox of the Cross

In stark contrast to the narcissism of our age stands another movement. Its symbol is a cross. Visualized to generations of children as a huge *I* with a line through it, the cross stands for the ego demanding its own fulfillment crossed out. Logically it is the antithesis of narcissism. Narcissism says, "Find yourself"; this movement says, "Those who lose themselves, find themselves." Narcissism says, "Be strong"; this movement says, "Those who are weak are the ones who have real strength in God." Narcissism says, "Enjoy life"; this movement says, "Those who die with Christ are the ones who really live." Narcissism says, "Money is the best revenge"; this movement counters by saying, "Those who give, are the ones who get; and paradoxically it is the poor who are the truly rich." "Be somebody," says the narcissist; but this movement says, "The least are the greatest, and the last shall be first."[20]

The gospel of this movement tells me that God himself died for me on a Roman cross two thousand years ago for no other reason than that he loves me. It makes the astonishing claim that everything that separates me from God was put on that cross, and that nothing I have done, am doing or ever could do can separate me from the love of God in Christ Jesus if I believe in the gift of God's Son. It announces to me that the broken body I see on that cross has taken the guilt of my warped human nature and all the sins I have committed into itself in order that Christ might bestow on me complete pardon and release. You and I could search the world for a philosophy that would guarantee self-esteem, but nowhere do we encounter one where the complete worth of the individual person is so affirmed as it is here. In the light of that cross I can finally relax my death grip on pride and egoism and discover by an act of faith that I really *am* somebody.

Uncomfortable as it sounds at first, there are no shortcuts to the joys of knowing God. He is known through the cross. Pseudo-Christianity will always tell you that there is another way to experience the Easter-type joy of new life apart from passing through the death of Good Friday. "Positive thinking," "Possibility thinking,"[21] some sudden and dramatic experience of the Spirit, a new kind of self-help therapy may all have much to say; but when they tell you that there is some way to get right into the joy without dealing radically with the self, they are offering a counterfeit gospel.

The gospel insists that what stands between humans and God is pride—the stubborn refusal to derive our worth from God's love alone. Until pride is dealt a fatal blow, there will be no authentic knowledge of God. Just as Alice had to be made small before she could become Alice in Wonderland, so it is only when there is humility at the starting point that there will be Truth at the end. Pride prevents us from seeing our desperate need for God. Just as it was true of Jesus' enemies, who had a superficial knowledge about God, pride becomes the root of our rage against a God who condescends to do for us what we cannot do for ourselves.

Jesus' most famous story was the parable of the Prodigal Sons. Contrary to what most people think, both sons squandered their inheritance: one with wine, women and song, and the other with stifling rectitude. The real hero of the story is the father who deals lovingly and patiently with both. The younger, demanding his inheritance, leaves home in a desperate search for self-fulfillment. For a while his dream comes true, but as he runs out of funds he finds he runs out of friends as well. Still confident of his own abilities, he finds work with a farmer who gives him the job—particularly odious for a Jew— of feeding his pigs! At last the lad is desperate enough to come to his senses, face his own inadequacies and sins, and return to his waiting father.

The older son, hearing the merriment surrounding the return of his scoundrel brother, remains at a distance. How could a father treat with such joy a son who had made such a mess of his life? A prisoner of his own pride, the older brother bitterly complains to his father and then wraps himself in a cloak of self-righteousness, refusing to respond to his father's invitation. His pride, wounded but not broken, prevents him from making the discovery of his life: that joy wins out in the end.

Jesus told the story to illustrate why it was that repentant sinners welcomed the reflection of God they saw in him, while the so-called righteous would have none of him. The story was intended to tell them that what stood between themselves and God was simply the pride they felt at not being sinners like others whom they condemned. As much in need of his love as any, these Pharisees were incapable of responding to joy because of their pride.[22]

The Power of the Cross

But how do we get beyond the cross as merely a powerful symbol of self-sacrifice? How do we get to the cross as a historical fact with a present dynamic message where ordinary people can lose themselves and then find themselves? How can a death two thousand years ago make such a radical difference to you and me today?

Christians have to confess an element of mystery here. While the message of the cross is puzzling and offensive to the skeptical mind today, it continues to have a power to change people that can only be ascribed to God himself.[23] The weight of personal testimony to this over the centuries is astounding. But what is its secret?

Part of the power of the cross comes from its unique ability to reveal at one and the same time the true character of God and the true character of ourselves. Jesus said "blessed are those who mourn," meaning in part that the capacity to feel things deeply is a prelude to great discoveries. Today one of our chronic problems is an inability to feel or to empathize. We watch a space shuttle explode before our eyes. What do we feel? Statistics of natural and manmade disasters around the world flood the evening news on TV. But who is really moved? One of our greatest needs is to be able to react emotionally to statistics. This inability to feel with or for others comes from our being out of touch with depths within ourselves that we cannot face.

But the message of the cross is that it was neither the Jews nor the Romans who really committed this ghastly action. Jesus, the man who had done nothing wrong, created the motive for his own death. It was our sin that made the cross necessary. Human resentment over the presence of incriminating purity put Jesus on the cross. Once we come to believe that we begin a lifelong thaw of the soul. The capacity to feel is awakened. We discover the freedom to mourn the warp in our own natures that caused God to take such drastic steps for our salvation.

What this amounts to is the freedom to admit about ourselves what everybody else already knows. The noted rector Sam Shoemaker once said to me of a very proper parishioner, "She has every virtue except a sense of sin."

The cross also reveals to us the character of God by demonstrating that God suffers with us. The theme of God's compassion is so imbedded in human consciousness that it keeps cropping up in the most unusual places. In his book *Night,* Elie Wiesel, prophet of the Holocaust, recounts the hanging of a Jewish youth in Auschwitz. The SS also hanged two older men with him. Fortunately for them, they died quickly. But the death throes of the youth lasted for a half hour. Other prisoners, forced to watch, groaned with sighs too deep for words, Wiesel writes, " 'Where is God now?' And I heard a voice in myself answer: 'Where is he? He is there. He is hanging there on the gallows.' "[24] In a way that perhaps Wiesel himself only partly understood, these words demonstrate that God suffers *in* our suffering.

But even beyond compassion, the cross reveals a God who suffers on our behalf. Although it is not fashionable in some circles to speak of Christ suffering our penalty as well as our pain, the New Testament makes the claim, in no uncertain terms, that the death of Jesus was a sacrifice for sin. What John Stott has called the "self-substitution of God"[25] is a theme running through both the Old Testament and the New.

In the rich imagery of both the Day of Atonement and Isaiah 53, Jesus found the meaning of his death as a vicarious sacrifice. "The Son of Man came to give his life a ransom for many" in one short phrase catches the overall meaning that Jesus ascribed to his death.[26] In what has sometimes been referred to as the great transaction, he took our sin on himself and gave us his righteousness in exchange. However, as John Stott points out, it was not our moral character that was transferred onto Christ on the cross, but rather the legal penalty that our sins justly deserved. "It is finished," Jesus' cry from the cross, was therefore not a sigh of defeat, but a proclamation of victory and satisfaction that the self-offering of God in Christ for our sin was acceptable.

While I believe it is important to highlight this aspect of the many-dimensional meaning of the death of Christ, it is important to emphasize that the cross was in no way a bare legal transaction. As the prophet Isaiah foretold, the one who would bear our sins would also bear our sorrows and our pain.[27] This has always been part of the true meaning of love.

A young girl had grown up with a mother whose hands were badly scarred. For years she was content to simply accept the fact that her mother's hands were different from all the other mommies' smooth hands. But as she grew older this difference became a source of embarrassment. Still she said nothing. But she began to feel great shame at the ugliness of those scarred hands. At the age of eight, she could finally stand it no longer, and out came the question: "Mommy, why do you have such ugly hands, when all the other mothers have smooth hands?" There it was, it was said. The young girl felt relief by just asking the question that had been in her mind so long.

Her mother quietly sat her down and told her this story: "When you were a little child, still sleeping in a crib, we had a sudden fire in the house, and when I went into your room, the flames were already around your crib. I grabbed you and wrapped you in a blanket. But the flames had already reached the outside of the blanket, and my hands, as you can see, were terribly burned. So, darling, that is why my hands are scarred and not lovely and smooth as other mothers' are."

There was a pause, and then a look of recognition came over the girl's face. She reached down and picked up her mother's hands in hers and held them tightly to her face. "Oh, Mommy, Mommy, I just love these hands."[28]

A third need we all have, beyond the need to see ourselves as we really are and to get a glimpse of God's extravagant love, is the need to make a commitment to something that is beyond ourselves. Yet bound by the egos we have tried to satisfy but have come to despise, we feel that such a commitment is impossible. Here again the gospel is good news. We are not asked to summon all our energies and make one herculean effort to commit ourselves. We are only asked to surrender our pride, come to God and say, "If you will take us as we are, faults and all, we are willing to bow before you." By this simple willingness, we find we are enabled to enter into a committed relationship with God.

For some, of course, the thought of such a bowing is unseemly. It is an indecorous groveling before a divine being too weak to admire and too vulnerable to worship. Such thoughts are not new. An early anti-Christian cartoon depicted a slave bowing before a crucified human figure with a donkey's head. The caption read: "Alexamenous worships his savior."

Some will never bend. They are stiff as ramrods. But Jesus Christ conveys a love that all who are willing to bend find irresistible.

Traveling through France, a small group of tourists were taken by the beauty of a Gothic cathedral. Pausing to tour the building, they were struck by the lovely rose window. Spotting a man in a cassock, who turned out to be the bishop himself, they asked if he would be willing to discuss some of the building's remarkable features. He was more than willing. One question he was asked was if there were any special stories connected with this cathedral. He said, "Yes, there are."

He then went on to tell of a group of tough boys in the city who many years before had formed a gang with a peculiar initiation rite. Before admission into the gang, every new recruit had to come to the steps before the high altar of this cathedral and say three times out loud: "Jesus Christ, you died for me, and I don't give a damn." There was one boy who greatly desired to join, so he entered the cathedral at night with a delegation from the gang. With a loud voice he managed to say, "Jesus Christ, you died for me, and I don't give a damn." But when he began to say it a second time, his voice faltered. He just couldn't get it all out, so he stopped. After looking at the other boys, he turned on his heels and ran from the cathedral. When the bishop finished the story, the tourists were obviously enthralled and asked the bishop whatever happened to the boy. The bishop paused for a moment and then said very quietly, "I was that boy."

The Joy of Dependence

Fourth and last, the cross creates a community of mutually dependent people who rejoice not in their autonomy, but in their companionship and their care for one another. The self does not survive in isolation, but desperately needs what the narcissist most dreads: dependence. Those who are spiritually united through a common surrender to the crucified one experience an ability to forge bonding relationships with each other that transcend natural ties. Real community thrives only when this kind of interdependence is not only permitted but openly celebrated. Conversely, the rejection of dependence causes the narcissist to embrace isolation.

I remember Dick as one of Harvard's gifted young oarsmen with a real strength in the double and single scull. When I first met him, he was sitting in his college dining room surrounded by friends who clearly recognized his talent. I was on campus to assist in a university mission with a noted evangelist. Surveying the dining room for a challenging group of students who looked least likely to be interested in Christianity, I had spotted Dick's crowd and asked if I could join. My worn tweed jacket was no disguise for the clerical collar I had decided to wear, and the group soon figured out why I had come to Harvard.

I discovered to my surprise that nearly all of them were planning to attend the mission, and they asked if I would join them. Doing my best to disguise my amazement and saying an unspoken prayer of thanks, I agreed with them on a meeting place from which to proceed to the auditorium.

The mission touched Dick deeply, and while there were still doubts and questions, what had been just an interest in Christianity matured into a solid determination to give it a try. He had been captured by the message of the cross. The following spring Dick and his roommate worked hard on their sculls in the hopes of qualifying for the Olympics to be held in Tokyo that summer. To encourage Dick I attended the final tryouts in New York City. The grandstand was full of friends, including Dick's proud parents.

Soon after the final race began, the race that would have qualified them for Tokyo, Dick and his roommate took the lead. We could see them coming toward us. Shortly they would be across the finish line. The crowd was going wild. But then, the unthinkable happened. Dick suddenly "caught a crab." His oar stuck in the water, and his boat came to a total standstill. The crowd gasped. Anxious instructions from Dick's father in the stands could be heard over the commotion. But it was all over. The other boat glided smoothly past them and over the finish line. The shame was overwhelming.

But the God whom Dick had met that past winter has a habit of turning failures into something good. Partly through the witness of other Christians over a period of time Dick was able to take a long look at himself in the light of the cross. He discovered paradoxically that losing can be winning if it enables us to recover the lost image of God in which we were all made.

Today Dick and his wife, Mardi, run a Christian community in Massachusetts where people discover the joy of interdependence and dependence on Jesus Christ. As I read through Dick's recent book, *Beyond Identity: Finding Your Self in the Image and Character of God,* I thought back to that day when I watched him blow his chance at the Olympics. I wonder if he could have written the book at all were it not for the lessons learned through that disappointment. He writes:

> The first step to resolve shame (is) to realize that God, through Jesus Christ, accepts you. Your . . . Father joyfully receives you with all your vanity, sin, and contradictions. God accepts the Christian whether the Christian accepts himself or not. Then one day he will replace our shame with its opposite—true glory and honor. . . . I can accept myself because God has forgiven and accepted me.[29]

Dick was freed, through dependence on Christ, to recover his true self and through that recovery to create a place where others are free to find their true selves. Skeptics may seek for reasons why all this could have happened naturally. But those who see the cross as neither foolish nor unnecessary, but in the words of St. Paul recognize it as "the power of God unto salvation" read quite another message. We hear the graceful word that once again it is possible to recover an ability to mourn, to feel deeply, to get in touch with the forces in us that led to the putting of the Son of God on a Roman cross. We hear a word of freedom, enabling us to know acceptance of the profoundest sort and equipping us to see even in life's disappointments opportunities to change and grow. We hear a word of victory that our sins are forgiven and fully paid for. And because we hear this message, the cross gives us a motive for doing what our nature both resists and cries out for: an opportunity to bow in surrender before a Greatness that invites intimacy. And then, almost as an unexpected gift at the end, we discover that by celebrating with others our dependence on God, rather than being ashamed of it, the cross overcomes our isolation and makes possible real community.

Then Moses answered, "But behold, they will not believe me or listen to my voice, for they will say, 'The LORD did not appear to you.' " The LORD said to him, "What is that in your hand?" He said, "A rod." And he said, "Cast it on the ground." So he cast it on the ground, and it became a serpent; and Moses fled from it. But the LORD said to Moses, "Put out your hand, and take it by the tail"—so he put out his hand and caught it, and it became a rod in his hand—"that they may believe that the LORD, the God of their fathers, the God of Abraham, the God of Isaac, and the God of Jacob, has appeared to you."   *(EXODUS 4:1-5)*

Catch a Snake by Its Tail
<u>The Agnostic's Refusal</u>

DURING FOGGY WINTER DAYS IN OXFORD, ENGLAND, AN inexpensive stew or pork pie at a local café relieves the boredom of the tasteless lunches dished up in college dining halls. Beautiful though the wood paneling and sculptured plaster ceilings in those dining halls are, and impressive though the portraits of notables and royalty are—for the student, lunch out is infinitely preferable to lunch in. So making a date to lunch out with a fellow student is a welcome interlude. I was delighted, therefore, when Dennis suggested that he and I take a break from the dining hall fare and meet at a local pub for a sandwich. Dennis had won a coveted Rhodes Scholarship from his native land, Australia, and, despite my lack of Commonwealth connections at the time, we both felt a kinship, being fellow students "from the colonies."

Dennis looked old for his age and at twenty-four was already balding. He was majoring in philosophy, politics and economics and headed for a career in law, leading eventually to public service. As we talked, he was quite frank about his religious agnosticism, knowing that I was a student of theology. During lunch he raised some objections to Australia's strict divorce law and asked me why I thought such a law had originally been enacted. I remember saying that I thought it was likely that the laws were based on British common law, which was in turn imbued with a Christian attitude toward the sanctity of marriage.

"But why should Christian attitudes be the foundation for laws?" he asked.

"Probably," I answered, "because people believed that Christian attitudes reflected the views of God himself."

Dennis pushed me. "Why should that be so?" We were soon onto a discussion of the divinity of Christ, which is exactly where Dennis wanted to take me.

Dennis had apparently not heard much about the claims of Jesus Christ or the evidence for his resurrection. I spent some time trying to spell them out, but I could tell I wasn't making much headway against his essentially skeptical cast of mind. We agreed to eat lunch together again and parted. I suspected that it was the last in-depth conversation we would have. But I was wrong.

Dennis could claim to stand in a noted tradition of Anglo-skeptics whose views have been exported around the world ever since what Cardinal Newman and William Gladstone termed "the great apostasy" of the late nineteenth century. It appeared to many that the 1870s in England saw, in the words of Matthew Arnold, a "revolution in religion." Indeed, one scholar has called the second half of the nineteenth century the period of the "death of God."[1]

Precisely because these years were so formative for the century that followed them, we need to understand some of the forces that were at work during this period. For agnosticism, as such, grew out of the confluence of certain ideas and movements which at first were only trickles but which eventually became a mighty river.

The Great Apostasy

The intellectual world of the late nineteenth century was studded with thoughtful conversions from orthodox Christianity to various non-Christian approaches to life. William Kingdon Clifford, noted mathematician, abandoned his high church Anglicanism; Sir Leslie Stephen, a writer, reared as an evangelical and an ordained clergyman, left the church for agnosticism. Charles Bradlaugh, son of a low-level clerk and a nurse, turned from orthodoxy to become a noted free-thinking editor and politician, spreading skepticism to the masses. George Eliot and Samuel Butler, both novelists, turned their backs on the faith. Butler, surveying a typical rural Church of England congregation commented that "they would have been equally horrified at hearing the Christian religion doubted [or] at seeing it practiced."[2] In the words of American author John Knowles, Christianity was taken by the average churchgoer as "a sort of abstract force for good, like nutrition."[3]

Nor was this intellectual revolt confined to Great Britain. Auguste Comte, the philosopher, and Ernest Renan, the historian, both in France; Jacob Burckhardt, the historian, in Switzerland; and David Friedrich Strauss, the dialectical philosopher, in Germany, were all a part of it too.

The impetus for this rejection of Christian orthodoxy came only in part from a disillusionment with the Victorian church. As Franklin Baumer outlines it, it came from several currents of thought that flowed together at this period of history to create a flood of objection to historic Christian belief.

One stream, which did relate to disillusionment with the Victorian church, was the rise of concern for social reform in the wake of the Industrial Revolution. The inequities between rich and poor, capitalist and laborer, slaves and freemen, women and men seemed to be perpetuated by the church's pronouncements of the blessedness of poverty and the justification of wealth as a blessing from God, as well as by the opposition the church exhibited to so-called free thought. In short, the church was seen as supporting the status quo. Christianity was lumped together with everything that stood in the way of progress, of openness to new ideas and of the betterment of humanity here on earth. James Mill, father of John Stuart Mill, looked upon religion as "the greatest enemy of morality."[4] His son, the popularizer of utilitarianism, insisted that no action or organization could be considered "good" if it did not promote the greatest happiness for the greatest number of people.

Another stream was the romantic era's fascination with the subjective side of human nature. The unconscious, with its dreams, fantasies and yearnings, became the focal point for literature, poetry and art, and for the rise of a new approach to religion. Although we immediately think of Freud in this context, he was not the first to locate the idea of religious "truth" in the subjective consciousness of man. It was the German Ludwig Feuerbach who thought it was out of our dreams and fantasies that religious notions arose. Deep within the psyche are needs and longings which call forth the "objects" of personal faith. It was Freud who some time later popularized this idea to the masses by linking the unconscious to a desire for a superhuman father. There were in fact many others at this time like Feuerbach and Freud who dissolved all belief in objective religious reality into the subconscious and the subjective.

A third stream was the new science of anthropology. Scholars eager to learn more about the myths and superstitions of our human past traveled to the far corners of the earth where primitive cultures still existed. The hope that drove them on was the expectation that in uncovering the symbols and rituals of uncivilized societies we could learn the origins of civilized religion. Sir James Frazer's _The Golden Bough_ (all thirteen volumes!) argued that because similar religious symbols were to be found in all cultures, they were not to be thought of as "true" or "false" but simply as part of the development of human thought.

Another stream in this mounting tide against orthodoxy was the rise of new economic theories rooted in Hegel's dialectic of thesis/antithesis/synthesis. According to Hegel, every movement produces a counter movement, which, in turn, leads to a third movement which, while appearing to be a resolution of the original tension, actually becomes a new thesis which prompts a new antithesis. As Karl Marx, Hegel's disciple, interpreted its meaning for economics: all history is a struggle between the dominating and the dominated classes (thesis); revolution by the oppressed is the only appropriate response (antithesis); a society free of exploitation, oppression and class struggles would be the result (synthesis).[5]

To Marx, another convert in reverse, religion was totally identified with the ruling class and was destined to be overthrown and disappear. What Marx did was to take Feuerbach's subjectivism and apply it not just to the individual, but to society. Religion was the product of a society that needed to uphold privilege and inoculate the underprivileged against revolt—or in Marx's well-known phrase, it was "the opiate of the masses." "The mortgage that the peasant has on heavenly blessings guarantees the mortgage that the bourgeois has on peasant lands."[6]

A fifth stream was the new breakthroughs in biological science. Until the late nineteenth century few people doubted the unique status of humanity in the universe. We were either created by God in his image or we were at least creatures unlike all other creatures because of our special capacity for reasoned thought. Through his two books, *The Origin of Species* (1859) and *The Descent of Man* (1871), Charles Darwin put an intellectual foundation underneath the emerging ideas of evolution and natural selection. Human beings, it seemed, were not the product of a personal God, but the end result of a long chain of events wherein the stronger forms of primitive life overcame the weaker and gave us what we see today. Gone was human uniqueness; gone was the idea of a purposeful design to the universe; and gone was the idea of rationality as yielding any truth other than what could be observed by the senses. As George Bernard Shaw put it: "We were intellectually intoxicated with the idea that the world could make itself without design, purpose, skill or intelligence: in short without life."[7]

These five streams—utilitarianism, romanticism, anthropology, Marxism and evolution—flowed together into a mighty flood tide of reaction to orthodox, biblical faith. To test whether there was any validity to what these men were saying, we have only to ask if these men are now universally thought to be wrong.

The Church in Reaction?

Do we need to deny that, out of fear of social and intellectual chaos, the church has often stood against reforms that were later acknowledged as greatly needed? Granted, this was, in part, out of a need to protect vested interests which were generally tolerant of churches as long as they stayed docile and didn't agitate. But that hardly makes it more acceptable. And what of Freud's analysis of the subconscious? Does it not contain many flashes of insight that we all accept today? Why, for instance, did my six-year-old daughter ask me not long ago whether it were possible, should her mother happen to die, for her to marry me? Haven't the anthropologists, by pointing out the superstitions and myths of earlier and distant cultures, shown how basically religious the human species is? And wasn't Marx right that the concentration of economic power in the hands of a few, without democratic safeguards and humane laws, leads to oppression and exploitation?

However, to see some truth in their positions is not the same as to accept all their conclusions uncritically. Few today would do so. It is true that some churchmen in the colonies sought to find a biblical basis for slavery, as some in South Africa justify apartheid today. But it was convinced Christians like Lord Shaftesbury and William Wilberforce, who were motivated by evangelical zeal, that led the battle for the abolition of slavery. In fact, it has been well documented that the religious revivals of the late eighteenth and early nineteenth centuries were the necessary precursors of the social reform movement of the later nineteenth century—that revivalism inevitably leads to social reform. It does so by kindling a zeal for perfection, which stimulates ethical behavior in all its dimensions, both individual and social.[8] Richard Lovelace writes of the impact of the Clapham Sect, that group of influential evangelical Christians committed to social change in nineteenth-century England:

> Lord Shaftesbury's efforts against the oppression of the British working class were simply the logical extension of the Clapham battle against slavery. Shaftesbury worked with other evangelical political leaders such as Richard Oastler and Michael Sadler to limit the abuses of child labor in industry and the mines, and worked also to improve the care of the mentally ill and the housing of the poor.[9]

Freud, Frazer, Marx, Darwin

Freud may have been right that young men subconsciously want to kill their fathers and marry their mothers. But most post-Freudians think his need to explain everything (art, religion, ethics, society) by sex tells us more about his obsessional neuroses than ours. The clients on whom Freud did his research were mostly middle class, middle age, middle income, Middle Europeans. Had he studied scullery maids in Liverpool, Hottentot tribesmen in southern Africa and panhandlers in Colorado, he might have reached different conclusions. Jung sought to correct Freud's fixation on the sexual drive and wrote: "Common-sense will always return to the fact that sexuality is only one of the life-instincts—only one of the psycho-physiological functions."[10]

James Frazer's illustrations of similarities between biblical teaching and ancient myths can argue *for* the truth of biblical teaching as well as *against* it. Are the myths of dying and rising gods found in ancient Near Eastern texts more true or less true because at a point in history God did send his Son to die and rise again? C. S. Lewis has argued that if the Bible's accounts are true, we would expect to find reflections of them throughout the conscious and subconscious myths of other cultures. "The heart of Christianity is a myth which is also a fact. . . . By becoming fact it does not cease to be myth: that is the miracle. . . . We must not be nervous about 'parallels' and 'pagan Christs': they *ought* to be there—it would be a stumbling block if they weren't."[11]

Marx was doubtless right that some have used religion to protect their privileges. But this game can be played by anyone. Voltaire is reputed to have once stopped an atheistic discussion at the dinner table, within earshot of his servants, out of concern for his silver! The use or misuse of an idea tells you nothing about its truthfulness. Marx seems to have made the mistake of thinking that if you can see how people have misused religion, its essential validity is thereby undermined. He took Feuerbach's views of Christianity lock, stock and barrel and apparently never analyzed the evidence for historical Christianity himself. No wonder current Communist propaganda still trots out the ridiculous assertion that Jesus was a mythological figure on a level with Woden and Thor![12]

Darwin pushed human antiquity way back before 4004 B.C., the date Archbishop Ussher determined in the seventeenth century by an overly literal reading of Genesis. But even Darwin recoiled at the idea, which soon became accepted evolutionary wisdom, that everything we know to be human and civilizing came from an impersonal origin by chance. "My theology is a simple muddle," said Darwin. "I cannot look at the universe as the result of blind chance, yet I can see no evidence of beneficent design, or indeed of design of any kind in details."[13]

In a sometimes humorously irreverent and skeptical treatment of science, David Berlinski, philosopher and mathematician, writes:

Chimpanzees do not talk, and apparently have nothing to say; they cannot read; they do not write; they do not paint, or compose music, or fashion sculpture; nor do mathematics, or metaphysics; they form no real communities, only loose-knit wandering tribes; they do not dine and cannot cook; there is no record of their achievement—not surprising, of course; beyond the superficial, they show little curiosity, they are born, they live, they suffer, and they die. . . . One may insist, of course, that all this represents only a difference of degree. One can also say that only a difference of degree distinguishes man from the Canadian goose.[14]

The fact of the matter is that we find little indication in the animal world of the powers of language, abstract thinking, artistic endeavor or moral reasoning that we associate with the human species. Can we really say that the difference between us and the animals is simply a matter of degree?

What I believe we are dealing with in these non-Christian systems are truths set in essentially false contexts. To admit limited validity on this or that point must not prevent us from calling into question the total framework in which that truth is placed. By the same token, I would never argue that biblical Christianity is true because, at this or that point, it speaks truths that we can accept because they happen to agree with a nonbiblical yardstick which we have determined to be true on some other basis.

The biblical world view is credible because it gives a coherent, consistent view of the world into which we can put "truths" learned from all the disciplines: science, psychology, art, literature, economics. It is true because it gives all that data (as well as data of its own) overarching meaning and significance. As C. S. Lewis so beautifully put it: "Christian theology can fit in science, art, morality, and the sub-Christian religions. The scientific point of view cannot fit in any of these things, not even science itself. I believe in Christianity as I believe that the Sun has risen not only because I see it but because by it I see everything else."[15]

Shame-Faced Atheists?

Nevertheless, the contemporary believer in orthodox Christianity grows up and is educated in a culture that has used a variety of methods to distance itself from biblical faith. The word we hear most widely used by those who have never had faith or who have lost the faith they had is *agnostic*. This word was first coined in 1869 by Thomas H. Huxley, the eminent scientist and humanist and grandfather of biologist Julian and writer Aldous. Thomas Huxley was surprised that the word stuck. It has, in fact, passed into common usage, meaning someone who "doesn't know" whether there is a God or not.

To Huxley only the senses could give us accurate knowledge. So it is impossible to know whether things beyond the senses are true or false. But as has often been pointed out, the term *agnostic* is misleading. While insisting that a permanent state of indecision must surround the truth or falsehood of religious truth claims, agnostics often seem quite certain that any such claims are not true. Huxley himself rejected as simply false, those views of God which he could not accept. He did not say: "I simply don't know." It seemed obvious to him what was not true and what was. For this reason committed atheists like Karl Marx's co-worker Friedrich Engels called the agnostics of his day "shame-faced atheists"—people who simply wanted a more comfortable label for their unbelief.[16]

The agnostic's challenge to the Christian believer is simply this: "You are committing intellectual suicide. You claim to know things that no one can know, for there is absolutely no empirical evidence to which you can point as proof. Where is the proof of the Trinity, divine providence, life after death, miracles and a host of other articles of Christian faith? By making such claims you Christians bring to a stop the all-important tasks of searching, questing and probing, which are the tools of the intellectual's trade."

Therefore, while some agnostics are genuinely open to the possibility of divine revelation and may find agnosticism a stepping stone to real faith, the majority see no possibility of religious knowledge. Their agnosticism is just as dogmatic as is the position to which they object.

A case in point is the eminent twentieth-century philosopher Bertrand Russell. In his book *Why I Am Not a Christian* he dissects religion and Christianity with a peculiarly unscientific bias. After enumerating cruelties done to humanity in the name of religion, which are sad but true, he rips a few sayings of Jesus out of context to show that Jesus was theologically wrong and morally defective. He finds particularly objectionable the fact that Jesus accused those who didn't care for his preaching of being a "generation of vipers." Russell claims that Jesus' teaching about the one unforgivable sin has caused untold misery to mankind.[17] But nowhere in Russell's writing do we find him seriously weighing the evidence, for instance, for the historicity and divinity of Christ, the miracles of Christ, or the historicity of the resurrection. As Colin Brown says "he conspicuously avoids coming to grips with biblical religion. . . . The serious reader who wants a balanced statement of the pros and cons is best advised to look elsewhere."[18]

Toward an Open Mind

The real reason agnostics refuse to consider the evidence for Christianity with an open mind is not that evidence is lacking. It is rather that they have accepted a faith that will not permit such a consideration. G. K. Chesterton put it this way:

> If it comes to human testimony there is a choking cataract of human testimony in favour of the supernatural. If you reject it, you can only mean one of two things. You reject the peasant's story about the ghost either because the man is a peasant or because the story is a ghost story. That is, you either deny the main principle of democracy, or you affirm the main principle of materialism— the abstract impossibility of miracle. You have a perfect right to do so; but in that case you are the dogmatist. It is we Christians who accept all actual evidence—it is you rationalists who refuse actual evidence being constrained to do so by your creed.[19]

It was to my Rhodes Scholar friend Dennis's credit that he was willing to examine the evidence. After our lunch together that day in the pub, we saw each other only for brief exchanges in the college quad or on the streets over a period of perhaps two months. But then Dennis suggested that we return to our pub for another meal. During lunch he carefully steered the conversation around to Australia's divorce laws, the validity of Judeo-Christian ethics, the divinity of Christ and finally to the evidence for the resurrection. He said, "I've read everything I could get my hands on, and I have a theory of my own." Surprised, I asked him to talk on. In the intervening two months Dennis had managed to read a variety of books seeking to interact with the biblical evidence for the resurrection of Jesus. Several were written from a decidedly skeptical point of view; but, no matter, he had seriously examined the evidence.

Dennis's reinterpretation of the New Testament data was clever: Jesus had not actually died, but only swooned in the tomb. Somehow he managed to get out into the night air and leave word with a prearranged messenger that he would meet his disciples in Galilee. Later, fully recovered from his ordeal, he met with them, convinced them that he had been victorious over death and sent them forth to tell the world that he was alive. Relying heavily on Hugh Schonfield's *Passover Plot,* which includes the novel twist that Jesus actually planned to fake death and through the help of an accomplice get himself out of the tomb and back to health, Dennis's thesis appeared to take the evidence of the New Testament seriously.[20]

But as I pondered his reconstruction it became obvious that far too many questions remained: How does one account for the official certification that Jesus had actually died? The spear wound in his side? The careful Roman guard at the tomb? The breadth and variety of the appearances of Jesus after his resurrection? The permanent transformation of the disciples and the emergence of a community which claimed—and has for two thousand years—that Jesus is still alive and present in their midst? I realized that Dennis had been much too selective in his treatment of the evidence and that what he had tried to do was to fit as many of the New Testament details as possible into a nonsupernatural view of the resurrection. Given the evidence, of which even in my student days I was aware, it seemed to me that Dennis had approached the material with a bias and had found what he was looking for.

Our choice in approaching the evidence for the resurrection appears to be between two views. One subjects reported historical accounts to an understanding of natural law that forbids the possibility of miracles. The other conceives of the possibility that unique historical events might change our ideas about natural laws. The issue for us is: Which has the final authority, natural law or history? Is it just arbitrary which view we choose to take? For instance, we might ask, did evolution happen because natural law determined that it would? Or did evolution happen merely as a series of historical events that lead us to deduce certain laws from what probably took place? In other words, do natural laws follow from and summarize historical events, or do they determine them in advance?

So much depends on our assumptions. As a third way through these seemingly irreconcilably opposite ways of looking at the world, the resurrection provides an alternative: Natural law does not operate apart from God to determine history. Nor does history operate as an absolute apart from God. Both natural law and history operate under God's sovereignty. This not only makes possible the resurrection, but it gives us its primary meaning as well.

Gaps in the Chain

This third way, of course, assumes a world in which not every event has an empirically verifiable cause—a world in which miracles are possible. The nineteenth-century skeptics and their successors came to believe that nature was a closed system. Nothing could enter it from the "outside." Their world view had the advantage of seeming to be entirely reasonable. It corresponded to what most people observe on a day-to-day basis, for it has to be confessed that few people see ghosts, touch miraculously restored limbs or "hear the rush of angels' wings." Furthermore, they lived at a time of wonder at what man could discover through the application of empirical investigation to the natural world; and they could see its amazing fruits in the benefits of the Industrial Revolution.

It was left to thinking people in the twentieth century to follow this world view to its eventual and logical conclusion: a determined universe where man is simply a cog in the wheel—one more effect in a long and ultimately purposeless chain of cause and effect. Writers like B. F. Skinner and Jacques Monod put the nails in the coffin of this view of human nature which stripped us ultimately not only of freedom but dignity and significance as well.[21]

But people protest this conclusion, and rightly so. In an effort to find a place for the transcendent dimension of life (truth, goodness, beauty), they have been looking to one or other of the various forms of monism that can be found. This permits them to agree that the universe is an interlocking machine, but to claim, nonetheless, that it is a divine machine. Or at least in the words of Arthur Koestler, they have said that there is a "ghost" that permeates the machine.[22] The monist route, while appealing to increasing numbers, is open to all the weaknesses I have described in chapter two, and in the end has to cope with the spectacle of a Hollywood actress like Shirley Mac-Laine proclaiming herself God.

There is, however, another way. Let us regard the mechanistic concept of a closed universe as simply one model through which to understand the workings of nature. Much of life fits into this model; but as Donald M. MacKay, formerly professor of communication in the University of Keele, points out from his studies on the human brain, not all. Imagine, he argues, that an observer, claiming to understand the workings of your brain, were to write an analysis of how you will act given this or that circumstance. If he knew *all*, then his prediction would (on a mechanistic model) be true. But what if you were to read his analysis and believe it? Would you not then have the freedom to choose to act as he predicted or not? Of course you would. But then, while the prediction would be true for him and true for you as long as you *did not know it*, it would no longer be true for you if you *did know* it. In fact, by believing it, you would make it wrong for him too! MacKay writes:

We thus arrive at the real mystery of what it is to be a man. . . . Current descriptions or predictions of any man's brain, if they go into sufficient detail, can in the end be said to be valid only from the partial viewpoint of the observer. In the very strongest sense they are invalid for the agent, and hence have no exclusive claim to be the "real truth" about his situation.

No complete prediction exists upon which he and the observer would be right to agree. I want to suggest that (the observer) would be right to believe that he has a decision to make, that it will not be made unless he makes it, that it will be made the way he makes it, and that he will be responsible for the way it is made.[23]

MacKay claims that this freedom does not derive from any physical gap in the chain of cause and effect within the brain, but rather a logical gap in the predictive process. And the reason for this is that while man *is* a machine, he is more than a machine as well. "I believe this kind of 'gap' is wide enough for all that biblical religion requires," he concludes. In other words, the mechanistic model is true as far as it goes. But it does not explain the whole of reality. If human beings, then, are free to choose and to act in nonpredictable ways, then the universe is not a closed system. All of which brings me back to the one, overarching claim of the New Testament: that God in his sovereign freedom, at one point in history, acted decisively to break the chain of cause and effect by raising Jesus Christ from the dead.

The Resurrection and History

The biblical writers leave us no doubt about the importance of the resurrection. All four Gospel writers end with ringing affirmations of its reality. In fact, can we imagine any of them bothering to write their story unless they believed it had happened? What would have been the point? For the early Christian preachers the resurrection was absolutely central, and for the apostle Paul it was of such fundamental importance that had it not happened our faith would be a sham.[24]

But what are the lines of evidence which might convince a modern agnostic with an open mind—that is, someone to whom it is possible that both history and natural law are subject to God? There is, first of all, the fact that the body of Jesus was gone. By dawn on the third day after the crucifixion visitors to the tomb found it empty. Reinforcements were sent to check out the story of the women who had arrived at the tomb early to add spices to the linen wrappings. Finding the tomb open and the grave cloths lying neatly in one place (as if a butterfly had emerged from its chrysalis), they found no trace of the body itself.

All four Gospel writers record the empty tomb and do so with enough significant variations of detail to convince an honest reader that they are not just giving an official party line. But it is not only their record that we have to go on, it is the fact that within a few short weeks (just over seven, to be exact) the disciples were proclaiming the resurrection of Jesus on the streets of Jerusalem to multitudes of eager listeners—and doing so right within earshot of the very people who had killed him. The Jewish or Roman authorities of the day had but one thing to do to squash the rumors: produce the body. But they obviously couldn't. The body was gone.

Because it is so often suggested, we must ask whether the disciples could have stolen the body. It is, of course, theoretically possible. But is it probable? Hardly. How many people would go to death as martyrs preaching with passion a message they knew to be false? Yet most of them risked their lives for their message. Does it seem logical that these men would go through the rest of their lives tenaciously preaching in public that Jesus was alive when they knew all along that his body was decomposing in a Christian hideaway somewhere?

As J. N. D. Anderson, director of the Institute of Advanced Legal Studies at the University of London, has written: "This would run contrary to all we know of them: their ethical teaching, the quality of their lives, their steadfastness in suffering and persecution." To this implausibility we must add another: the disciples were not expecting the resurrection. Michael Green points out in *Man Alive* that in the postcrucifixion depression that they all felt, their only thoughts were to "run away, hide, and forget all about the whole affair. . . . They had no thought of carrying on his cause. Resurrection never entered their heads."[25]

We must conclude that for the Romans or the Christian disciples to have stolen the body is extremely improbable. Nothing was done to produce the body when belief in the resurrection was sweeping the city. Another theory is that Jesus could have survived the crucifixion and, along the lines of Dennis's suggestion, convinced his friends that he had been victorious over death. But this, as I have pointed out, strains credulity to the limit.

After all, he had suffered a forty-eight hour ordeal of three trials and scourging by the deadly cat-o'-nine-tails (people had been known to die of that alone). He had received no nourishment and undergone an excruciating crucifixion, which included a deadly wound to his side. Then he had been wrapped in tight gravecloths. Are we to believe that, even with assistance, he could have endured all that, gotten through a two-thousand-pound slab door, breaking its Roman seal, and walked past the highly trained and disciplined Roman guard to stumble into Jerusalem and convince his followers that he had risen to a new and glorious life? Only someone with a passionate commitment to the nonexistence of the supernatural would venture to say so.

Close Encounters

The appearances of Jesus following his resurrection form a second line of evidence. Each of the Gospel writers cites some of these appearances,[26] but it is Paul in 1 Corinthians 15:1-8 who lists them in order and mentions three appearances the others omit: to James (the Lord's brother), to himself on the Road to Damascus and to five hundred believers on one occasion. It is hard to assert that these appearances were later embellishments by pious believers and not actual eyewitness accounts when you consider how early the tradition of these appearances was circulating in the Roman world. Paul, writing to the Corinthians between A.D. 52 and 57, reminds his readers that he has already given them a verbal account of what he was writing to them about the appearances of Christ. That takes us back to Paul's first visit to Corinth, about A.D. 50.

But what did he tell them then? He says in 1 Corinthians 15:3 that what he shared with them at that time was a tradition he had himself received from the apostles. But when had he received this tradition? Back in A.D. 35 when Paul made his first visit to Jerusalem to confer with Peter and James, leaders of the Jerusalem church! In the letter to the Galatians, certainly one of the earliest books of the New Testament, Paul gives some of the details of that visit and mentions the agreement between what he was preaching and what these leaders believed.[27] What this shows is that the tradition about Jesus, especially his death and the details of his resurrection appearances, was firmly established within a decade, at the most, of the crucifixion.

Most of us who were teen-agers or older on November 22, 1963, remember not only the details of the assassination of President John F. Kennedy, but the very spot where we first heard the news. Imagine for a moment that some time later we heard rumors that people were claiming that he was not dead, but had come alive again and was making appearances to various individuals and groups. Imagine that we had heard that virtually every member of his former Cabinet claimed to have seen him and was giving speeches about it all across the country. Then we hear that some five hundred Democratic Party members at a banquet say they saw him; and now to top even these reports, his archrival Barry Goldwater has become a believer! Wouldn't you check these reports out? Furthermore, if Kennedy had promised in various speeches before his assassination that he would be shot and would rise again, wouldn't it add significantly to your curiosity?

In establishing the historical validity of any event, eyewitness accounts are held to be of the greatest importance. But, some argue, these were just hallucinations—the excited and yearned-for imaginings of women like Mary Magdalene? But consider the fact that people don't have hallucinations at different times and in different places. Nor do five hundred people all see a hallucination at the same time. Yet Paul writes that most of that group of five hundred were still alive at the time of his writing to confirm his report.[28]

The third line of evidence that points to an actual resurrection from the dead is the transformation that took place among Jesus' followers. Such a radical change as theirs must have had a cause. Within a few short weeks, eleven dispirited men, crushed by the loss of their teacher and ready to go back to their former professions, suddenly become avid, enthusiastic, utterly unshakable advocates of a resurrected Lord. It makes you wonder.

Then when these sincere Jews fundamentally alter their approach to sacred traditions, you see the impact of the resurrection on their entire world view. Within a few years they had changed their holy day from Saturday to Sunday—the day he rose. Their worship in synagogue and Temple now became a fellowship meal in which their risen Master was claimed to be present in a special way. Their initiation rite changed from circumcision to baptism in which new believers ceremonially die and rise again with Christ. Would these changes have happened if these men and women had not become unshakably convinced that Jesus was alive again?

A Lawyer's Probings

Some years ago a London lawyer named Frank Morison began to write a book about the last days of Christ, believing him to have been a great prophet who was martyred—but nothing more. As he sifted the evidence, he found his skepticism disappearing before the trustworthiness of the New Testament record. In the end he wrote a book aimed at proving the resurrection and appropriately entitled the first chapter: "The book that refused to be written."

Like Frank Morison, I can vividly recall my own dawning realization of the power of the resurrection. I was seventeen and off at a New

England boarding school. It was the beginning of spring term. I had for some time been curious about the claims of the New Testament; and so one night after lights were out, I descended the narrow spiral stairway that led from my dormitory through a tower into the darkened chapel. The only light came from a flickering candle hanging over the altar area. I sat in the chair reserved for the headmaster and glanced down the long expanse of empty pews pondering the meaning of Easter. It wasn't that I had ever disbelieved the resurrection, but it had meant no more to me than a nice story. Jesus must have risen, and I assumed that he then simply disappeared again presumably to die a quiet, natural death.

But as I sat there in the dark for perhaps a half an hour the thought came to me that if Easter was more than just a pious myth, it had to mean that Jesus was still alive and that, if that were true, I could actually communicate with him now in a personal way. A deep sense of peace came over me as my mind gradually awakened to a mysterious presence who had been with me all along. Of course, the resurrection cannot be proven. But the evidence is truly overwhelming to anyone who will examine it with an open mind.

To the agnostic who claims that there is only one way to know anything, we must say: "Be more scientific, not less." It is reductionist to insist that there is only one way to know. In mathematics knowledge proceeds, not from hard facts, but from axioms. In personal relationships knowledge proceeds from encounter with other people. We must make room for more than one way of knowing. When historical evidence combines with personal encounter, we find ourselves believing in a risen Christ and also in a world view big enough to hold all the facts.

A Radical's Faith

By a unique series of circumstances in 1968 I found myself chaplain to the historic little Anglican parish of St. Peter's, Zermatt, Switzerland. In the predominantly English congregation one Sunday morning a face stood out. The young man had long, blond hair in the fashion of the sixties, and he was listening to my sermon with the kind of intensity that is every preacher's wish. The sermon contrasted the hope of the gospel with the lack of hope found in contemporary culture. I felt it was too full of quotes from gloomy existentialist writers like Camus, Sartre and Beckett. But it turned out that these were precisely the authors that this young man had been reading in search of answers to the fundamental questions of life.

Bob came to see me that afternoon in the little hotel where my wife and I were staying. For two hours he drilled me with questions about Christianity. He told me he had been president of S.D.S., the radical Students for a Democratic Society, at Harvard in the sixties and had then dropped out of college following a bitter demonstration he led against the university in front of the president's house. The sudden and dramatic experience of power he felt as the leader of that demonstration precipitated an intellectual crisis within him during which he became aware that he had no basis for the values in which he so passionately believed. Once out of college he began heavy experimentation with drugs in an attempt to discover meaning in a world where there were just too few handles to grasp. Bob took off for Europe and based himself in Stockholm. For several months he backpacked and hitchhiked everywhere, spending his idle moments reading authors whose view of reality ended in absurdity and despair.

It was the church bells that morning and the desire to hear some English spoken that caused him to wander into St. Peter's. Our conversation that afternoon was only the beginning. Bob left Zermatt, went to the L'Abri community nearby at my suggestion and subsequently began reading the New Testament. But drawn though he was to real faith, doubts flooded through his mind as he sought to reconcile his agnostic assumptions with the answers he was hearing and reading.

Finally, he realized that he had been wanting God to convince him of the truth of Christianity before he decided to embrace it. From his "objective" perspective this all seemed quite reasonable. But he came to see that his unwillingness to submit to the truth (if it was so) was one of the main obstacles in the way of his ever discovering it. So late one night that spring he prayed: "Lord, if you're there, you can convince me that you're there. I don't know what it will take, but if you are truly God, you can do it. And, Lord, I know that I am supposed to pray, give my life to you and then follow you. I can't pray that. I'm not together enough to promise you my life. . . . But if you are God, you can enable me to do that." Bob writes: "As I finished praying, there were no trumpets, no writing on the wall, just an incredible sense of peace and assurance that God was there. Since then I have had a real conviction that has never been shaken that Christianity is true."

Returning to Cambridge, Bob graduated, went to theological seminary, was ordained, ran a drug-and-alcohol agency for the State of Maryland, and then pursued public service as an elected representative in the state assembly. Bedrock to his life is the conviction that to understand the logic of the gospel, one's heart must be open to the truth.

Black Village

Walking through the worst slum in the Bahamas was for me a study in contrasts. Just a short distance away are the luxury hotels that line fashionable Cable Beach, but here on both sides of the dusty streets of Nassau's Black Village were the signs of depression, defeat and death. In the middle, under the shade of an old tree, was a tumbledown shack called the "crack house," where residents of all ages forgot their troubles for a few hours, thanks to the new concentrated form of cocaine which in the early eighties was flooding Nassau and was soon to hit the North American market. I noticed only one house that was well kept up and learned that it belonged to the local representative of the Bahamian Mafia—the Village's supplier.

My friend David Allen, a respected island psychiatrist who has taught at both Harvard and Yale, together with several other Christians had opened a ministry of care and hope for the people of Black Village. They served free open-air breakfasts weekly and supported a couple who felt called to live among the people there as a sign of God's love and concern. "Hello, Doctor," people called, as we walked slowly down the lanes. A small group followed us into a simple cement structure where about fifteen folding chairs had been arranged in a circle. We sang a few songs, and then each one in the room shared a bit of their story. One, an exprostitute and drug addict, told of her struggle to come clean. Another said he was still unemployed, but had been drugfree for a whole year now. Each one had some word of gratitude to offer to God. And then I took the loaf of bread and the cup of wine on the small table in front of me, said a simple prayer of thanks and passed the elements around. Few words needed to be said, because we all sensed that in the midst of death, the risen Christ was known.

Alongside the agnostic's assertion that no one can know the truth must be placed centuries of testimony like Bob's and the believers in Black Village to an encounter with the living God. Can agnostics be certain that all these people are wrong? To Blaise Pascal the issue was simple. This seventeenth-century scientist/mathematician/philosopher argued that each of us must wager. Although we cannot see God and cannot prove the truth of the gospel to the exclusion of all possible doubt, we must nevertheless gamble our lives on the possibility that it might be true. When we do, we discover that "the heart has its reasons which are unknown to reason."[29]

When Pharaoh drew near, the people of Israel lifted up their eyes, and behold, the Egyptians were marching after them; and they were in great fear. And the people of Israel cried out to the LORD; and they said to Moses, "Is it because there are no graves in Egypt that you have taken us away to die in the wilderness? What have you done to us, in bringing us out of Egypt? Is not this what we said to you in Egypt, 'Let us alone and let us serve the Egyptians'? For it would have been better for us to serve the Egyptians than to die in the wilderness." And Moses said to the people, "Fear not, stand firm, and see the salvation of the LORD, which he will work for you today; for the Egyptians whom you see today, you shall never see again."

(EXODUS 14:10-13)

When Your Back's to the Wall
The Pragmatist's Wager

ALTHOUGH PRAGMATIC THINKING IS AS AMERICAN AS APPLE pie, pragmatism as a philosophical system has long outlived its day. Founded in the late nineteenth century by Charles S. Peirce and popularized by William James, pragmatism was rooted in the idea that before you determine the truth of any idea you must have asked the question: "Does it work?" Truth was not to be viewed as a stagnant concept, inherent in the idea itself. It "happened" to an idea when it was proven to be true by subsequent events. If you could assimilate an idea, validate it in your experience and then corroborate it with the experience of others, then and only then were you entitled to say that it was true. To the pragmatist ideas are not right or wrong until they are unpacked for their practical consequences.

As a philosophy, pragmatism fitted well into the growing subjectivism of the late nineteenth century and the new fascination with evolution. Not only had life evolved, ideas are constantly evolving too. Truth is not absolute and fixed, but it needs perpetual criticism and re-evaluation. Ethical perspectives and value commitments need alteration as people's experience and knowledge grows and develops. Anything doctrinaire and dogmatic, anything closed to the ever-changing nature of truth is fanatical. The person who is really devoted to truth is the person on a continual search, the person open to new ideas, the person with a free and inquiring mind, who is conscious of how relative his or her own view of the world must necessarily be.

While pragmatism as a philosophy is now intellectual history—as an *ism* it must now be considered a *wasm*—the basic ideas which its promoters fought for have filtered down to the masses and today form part of the common-variety doubter's arsenal against the claims of absolute systems, especially the absolutes of biblical Christianity.[1]

Because pragmatic assumptions are so pervasive today, many Christians present the gospel message as believable not because it is true, but because it is workable. Although I hear that their private teachings are more in conformity with Christian orthodoxy than what gets quoted in public, popular preachers like Norman Vincent Peale ("Positive Thinking") and Robert Schuller ("Possibility Thinking") ride to popularity on a presentation of Christianity as the best "self help" prescription available. Dale Carnegie's *How to Win Friends and Influence People* continues to merge Christian principles with pragmatic assumptions. Books with titles like *Prayer Works* or *It's Better to Believe* are efforts to cash in on a pragmatism still latent in our culture, while often not giving a coherent rationale for why Christianity is not only helpful but true.

But Can She Type?

In his most popular work *Varieties of Religious Experience,* William James explored healthy and unhealthy expressions of the spiritual life. Because he discovered that for many people religious ideals do "work," he was willing to make room for the "validity" of particular religious and ethical viewpoints, as long as they were held to be only relatively true. But his positive attitude toward religion and religiously based ethics was not an endorsement of the eternal validity of such views.

To the contrary, because everything is changing, yesterday's "truth" may be tomorrow's "falsehood." It was axiomatic to James that our view of the world is provisional, temporary, tentative, partial and perpetually open to correction and falsification. "Our ethical commitments and our value perspectives may require alteration as our experience and knowledge grow and develop."[2] Ideas are never useful because they are true. They are true because they are useful.

It should be noted that James's theory ignores the possibility that some people might find false ideas useful. False ideas of "love" have been profoundly useful tools in the hands of twentieth-century "truthmakers." Susan Atkins claimed at the murder trial of Sharon Tate that the killing in which she participated was "all coming out of love."[3] Radio Hanoi early in 1980 interpreted the Russian invasion of Afghanistan as "an action of generosity and love to humanity,"[4] and from otherwise rational people one hears that the infanticide of handicapped newborn babies is justified as compassionate because it is "in their best interests"!

Pragmatism was yet another way of saying that truth is relative. But the unique twist it gave to relativism was this: Truth is relative to its intended results. John Dewey, noted educator and pragmatist, whose views still underlie most public education in North America, claimed that the ultimate goal of life was growth. One never arrives, achieves perfection or grasps a fixed truth. Since people continually grow, ideas do too. In other words, "To travel hopefully is better than to arrive."

Today modern pragmatists are not likely to know much about their intellectual forbears. Though they are likely to be tolerant of religion for those who need it and perhaps quite aware of the benefits of sincere faith in everyday experience, today's pragmatists for the most part regard religion as a crutch for those who are emotionally wounded. The idea that religion might have truth claims that bear investigation and demand decision does not cross their minds. The only test to apply to an idea is that of practicality. Does it work? Does it help you get ahead? Does it win you friends? Does it solve any of life's real problems? Or, does it do the opposite: compound life with a truckload of problems of its own?

The immediate reaction of modern pragmatists to believing Christians is negative. Believers are simply not seen as growing, searching, open-minded individuals, eager to test truth wherever it is found. Rather they are seen as ascetics, people with narrow interests and limited pleasures, persons with an obligation to live lives of self-denial and costly altruism. In the light of this, pragmatists ask, How can Christianity work for me?

The Cost of Discipleship

Dietrich Bonhoeffer was a towering young figure in Europe between the two world wars. As a brilliant theologian, he had taught and was honored at universities and schools on both sides of the Atlantic. He took a courageous stand and became a part of the resistance to Hitler out of Christian conscience and then participated in the plot to assassinate Hitler. He was caught, imprisoned and on April 9, 1945, executed by the Nazis. Prior to his imprisonment, in response to a question about what it really means to be a Christian, he had replied: "When Jesus bids a man follow him, he bids a man to die."

It is futile to try to dismiss the pragmatist with pious phrases about "abundant life." Real Christian commitment is always the "way of the cross." There is no padded pew for real Christianity. Many don't like to hear it, and preachers often gloss over it, but discipleship is costly. There is no "cheap grace." Most of Jesus' closest followers paid for their commitment with their lives. Millions more have done so ever since. In the twentieth century alone there have been more martyrs for the Christian faith than in all previous centuries combined![5] While self-styled ascetics may portray what we feel to be a distorted vision of how Christians interact with the world, there is no getting around the fact that serious Christians by their allegiance to Christ are called to live in a creative tension with the powers of this age.

When judged by the standards of our affluent, Western, self-oriented culture, committed Christians often look like oddities. Beneath the surface, they have different values, different personal goals in life and different standards from those of their neighbors. Paradoxically, although their Master gave them peace, he promised them tribulation.[6] W. A. Pevey, in a poem that later became a hymn, cited the sufferings of the first apostles and concluded:

This peace of God, it is no peace,

But strife closed in the sod.

Yet, brothers, pray for but one thing—

The marvelous peace of God.

While we must frankly admit the tough side to discipleship, modern pragmatists ought to see that they set the frame of reference within which they test the workability of ideas too narrowly. In other words, our claim is that the problem with pragmatists is that they are not pragmatic enough! Look at four areas of human experience and ask if pragmatists have adequate answers.

The Final Test

Benjamin Franklin's epigram that "in the world nothing is certain but death and taxes" points to the need for everyone to come to terms with the fact of death. In a new book entitled *The Hour of Our Death,* French cultural historian Philippe Aries maintains that one of the dominant features of death in the twentieth century is that it is invisible. Because death is denied, we lie to the dying about their condition and the dying lie to us and to themselves. We put the dying in hospitals not only to reduce their suffering, but also to reduce ours. Mourning is private. Grief is discouraged. Why don't we want to deal with death? Because in a materialistic age, death is the ultimate indecency.

Yet death is everywhere. In the United States someone dies every seventy-two seconds. The number of people killed by automobile accidents, homicides, terrorist activities and suicides rises every year. In the last twenty-five years suicide has tripled among adolescents. An average of eighty Americans kill themselves every day. But despite the fact of death how pragmatic are most people about their own death? It seems likely that people do not want to think about it because they cannot think beyond it. In John Steinbeck's *The Winter of Our Discontent,* Ethan Allen Hawley philosophizes about why his wife, Mary, is able to sleep so soundly and why he fights sleep.

> I have thought the difference might be that my Mary knows she will live forever, that she will step from the living into another life as easily as she slips from sleep to wakefulness. She knows this with her whole body, so completely that she does not think of it any more than she thinks to breathe. Thus she has time to sleep, time to rest, time to cease to exist for a little. On the other hand, I know in my bones and my tissue that I will one day, soon or late, stop living and so I fight against sleep, and beseech it, even try to trick it into coming.[7]

Again and again this contrast is borne out in the Christian's experience. A young Dartmouth College graduate I knew had to leave the boys' boarding school where he was a very popular teacher in order to come home to die of cancer. Peter and I talked several times. Through the witness of his sister and some friends, Jesus Christ became real to him. During the months when chemotherapy raised hopes only to be quickly dashed, I noticed that a Bible his friends had given him was a constant companion. Peter faced death bravely. Not for a minute would I minimize the tragedy of his death. But because of his faith, it was followed by a joyous funeral which transformed the occasion from mourning into a celebration of eternal life.

Another young man, whose family are close friends and who was a ranking East Coast tennis player from Swarthmore College, also struggled with terminal cancer. Shortly before he died he recorded these thoughts on tape:

> If one wants to find meaning, one need look no further than God and once one has found that and grasped that and refuses to let go of it, there is meaning in everything and it extends forever. . . .

Each thought I record may be my final one, but I feel God is there. He has given us free will, but he also is very much guiding my life and he has given me the reasons for living the way I have. I am who I am through the grace of God.

History knows of no antidote to the terrors of death except the message of victory found in the empty tomb of Jesus. Through the ages it evokes confidence in the face of tragedy and replaces fear with calm trust. Maria, a Russian nun, voluntarily walked with a terrified Jewish girl into the gas chamber at Ravensbruck because, as she said, "Christ is risen—there is nothing to fear."

The Purpose of Suffering

Modern pragmatists also have a problem with suffering. There is the temptation to fatalism on the one hand and the temptation to escapism on the other. From the Stoics onward can be found a common attitude to suffering: "Grit your teeth and bear it. Don't ask questions. Suffering is part of a world determined by impersonal, uncaring fate." The alternative seeks to escape suffering. Troubles are either drowned in a glass (or two) of Jack Daniels or wished away through meditation or denial. In the spectrum of world religions Islam is closest to the former because everything, including all suffering, is directly the will of Allah. Buddhism, on the other hand, is closest to the latter because if you follow the eightfold path, it is promised that you will avoid suffering and attain Nirvana.

But the Bible excludes these two options. It certainly is not fatalistic, for God creates us with freedom. Thus while God allows suffering, it is not his sovereign action; it is the result of our inhumanity toward one another. A God who would make human beings in such a way that they would not have the freedom to choose to create a slum or a concentration camp, or to harness atomic power for evil would have created puppets—not persons.

Nor is the Bible escapist. Because the God of the Bible cares so much for the world which he has made, he takes the world's suffering to himself, entering into that world to lift the full weight of its suffering upon his shoulders and transform it into the means whereby we might find our wholeness. The apostle Peter, quoting the Hebrew prophet Isaiah, writes: "By his wounds you have been healed."[8]

The proper question for the Christian then is not "How can I accept suffering?" Merely to accept it implies resignation or fatalism, just as the question "How can I avoid suffering?" implies escapism. Our question is always: "What shall I suffer for?" The fact is that all will suffer to one degree or another—some will suffer excessively, others much less. The basic issue is the ultimate goal in our lives which makes our suffering either despairing or redemptive. Christians are pragmatic about suffering because they have a goal in life big enough to suffer for.

In *Ah, But Your Land is Beautiful,* South African Nobel Prize-winning author Alan Paton tells of a man faced with the cost of making a commitment with life-and-death consequences. If he chooses as he believes, he will suffer at the hands of his opponents and be ostracized by his friends. Paton's Christian presuppositions emerge in the man's reply:

> I don't worry about the wounds. When I go up there, which is my intention, the Big Judge will say to me, "Where are your wounds?" and if I say, I haven't any, he will say, "Was there nothing to fight for?"[9]

Confusion of Goals and Objectives

Lacking a framework for discovering a sense of ultimate purpose, because there is no absolute truth, the pragmatist thirdly shows a tendency to mistake objectives for goals. A student poll on life goals revealed this confusion: My goals?

☐ to get a college education with good grades
☐ to become a respected actress
☐ to become wealthy

☐ to build a computerized house that is at least 75% independent
   of power sources

☐ to be successful at everything I do

☐ to make it in sports; to marry; to write some books

My point is not to quarrel with these if they are short-term objectives, but they illustrate the confusion that exists between goals and objectives. A proper life goal should never change. Objectives will continually change, especially if they are reached and accomplished. Even the goal of "success" needs further amplification because of its strict monetary interpretation in our society. Gaining "respect" and "making it in sports" have their obvious appeals as objectives, but they too can be very short-lived. Can they serve as ultimate goals? In the poem "To an athlete dying young," the final stanza indicates how ephemeral earthly honors are. Speaking as if to the departed young athlete, A. E. Housman writes:

Now you will not swell the rout
Of lads who wore their honors out,
Runners whom renown outran
And the name died before the man.

Small consolation, says the cynic. But would it not have been better to set one's sights higher than the honor itself? Those who believe in Jesus Christ and set as their ultimate life goal to enhance his reputation, rather than their own, display a more pragmatic approach to purpose.

What was it that motivated an Eric Liddell to leave the Paris Olympics and spend the remainder of his life as a missionary in China? His answer would have been that he sensed "His pleasure" whether running in Paris or teaching in Tientsin. To please God remained Liddell's foundational life goal, whether rescuing a dying man alongside a Buddhist temple or telling about the kingdom of God to simple people in the villages. He wrote, "I never had so much joy and freedom in my work as here."[10]

What is it that leads the headmistress of a girls' school in India to leave the comfort of her cloister and go out among the poor and dying of Calcutta? Fame was the last thing in Mother Teresa's mind. Her life purpose has remained steady: to serve Jesus Christ by serving the poor. What factors beyond personal ones led three-term governor and esteemed U.S. senator Harold Hughes to decide not to run again for the U.S. Senate so that he could work quietly behind the corridors of power in Washington, as a layman, to strengthen the Christian witness of men and women in positions of responsibility? It was known to Hughes's friends and acquaintances that he was motivated by a life goal that could not be satisfied by human achievements.

I can hear so many students whom I encountered in my twenty-five years of school-related ministry responding that the need for a religious goal in life is "some kind of a crutch." Fearing dependencies of any kind, our modern young idealists are driven to see purpose primarily in selfish terms. But people need crutches because humankind is limping! A glance at today's newspaper or an honest look at the everyday lives of people around us should convince us that this is true. If so, then a crutch is needed, isn't it? People of course choose crutches all the time, but some are ones to lean on and others are ones to get them moving. Those who can't celebrate without a six-pack of Michelob, or play sports without winning, or make it through an academic year without a boyfriend or girlfriend, or control their eating habits, or get through winter without a Bahamas tan, or face a day without three cups of coffee and a pack of Camels are using crutches to lean on.

Jesus Christ engenders the sort of dependency that moves one out in genuine concern for others and paradoxically also meets our own deep-seated need for a purpose greater than ourselves. Macho independence may have a superficial attractiveness to those who are young and idealistic, but as a goal for life it is a dead end. As others have said, there is no smaller package than a person all wrapped up in himself.

The Challenge of High Adventure
Conservatism and adventure are not usually linked in the popular

mind. But there is more than one kind of conservatism. There are self-styled liberals who follow the trends, simply going along with the present currents in society. They may think of themselves as liberal or even radical, but their essential mark is conformity to the culture's drift at any given time. Real conservatism, however, seeks to lay hold of an essential core of truth and then risks all—even the disapproval of those who are following current trends—in order to implement it.

In the 1960s Jerry Rubin was almost synonymous with radicalism. Marching to the revolutionary tune of the "Yippies," he accused the system of corruption and became an advocate for hedonism in his book *Do It*. He had a vision of significant change in society. But where is Rubin today? Today he works behind the desk of a major Wall Street brokerage firm selling tax shelters to chic young investors. He is also getting into the high-class restaurant business. Perhaps Rubin realizes that the moral differences between idealism and materialism are not as great as he once thought. As Paul Johnson, focusing on the convergence of idealism and materialism, asks: "Where exactly is the moral order of precedence among young graduates who want to pursue a career in politics, or take a desk job in a *well-financed 'public interest'* organization like Amnesty International, or who intend to set up in business?"[11]

The *New York Post* called the 1960s and early 1970s radicals "flaming moderates" with good cause. Despite all their anger at the complacency of the society around them at the time, were they not trendy conservatives who conformed to the drift of their day, which in due time spent its course? Once they entered their thirties and forties, they began to conform to the very materialism they criticized. I am reminded of a statement made by Harold Macmillan: "We all begin by being radicals, but end up by becoming firm members of the establishment." Perhaps not all, but enough to indicate a trend.

In my experience the call to high adventure does not come again and again in life. There are peak moments when we are particularly susceptible. Major transition moments, such as that from high school to college, are such times. In the winter term of my senior year at an all-boys' New England boarding school, I accepted an invitation to accompany six or seven others in my class on a midwinter weekend in New York City. Once there I regretted my decision because it was clear that the purpose of the evening's events was to get as inebriated as possible.

The waitress took our orders for drinks. Wisely for business that evening she failed to ask for our ID cards, for we had none—at least none that would certify us as 18—the mandatory drinking age in New York in those days. Sitting at a crowded table I began to feel strangely alienated from my friends and didn't like the fact that even if I wasn't going to drink, I would have to pay a stiff cover charge anyway. Peeved that I wouldn't join them at the altar of Bacchus, one of the guys made the suggestion that I could stand at the bar and watch the floor show without paying any cover charge. So I stood at the bar.

Up to a mike on a dingy little stage sashayed a woman of mammary distinction who was wearing a long dress and had heavily made-up eyes. In a throaty voice she began to belt out a song which was popular in the forties and fifties, long before the word *gay* came to have its modern associations:

Come on, get happy;
come on, get gay;
Come on get happy;
get ready for the judgment day.

As if it were yesterday, I can remember the thoughts going through my mind that cold January evening at the Lido Bar on 52nd Street. What would it be, Peter, a life of conformity to what was expected of me by my friends—perhaps my family? Where would it lead? To Wall Street? To a city bank? To business? But just as clearly as I could see that expected path, I could also see an alternative. It was a life of adventure and risk—a life of attempted obedience to a God I was only dimly coming to know. Although these were the alternatives, at the time it didn't seem a choice. I quickly put on my coat, bid good night to my friends and stepped out into the night air. For a long time I just walked the streets of New York City, pausing from time to time to glance up into the bright starlit night. I was conscious of having made a fundamental life choice and, although I knew it was a choice few would understand, I knew I had discovered a purpose that would be with me all my days.

My reading of the Gospels convinced me that consistently Jesus chose the path of adventure. Mild religious types were simply not drawn to him. In fact, they were offended by his call to radical commitment. Nor, curiously enough, were the extremely religious interested in him, for they already "had their reward" in the respectful adulation of the crowds.[12] They had found a way to "make religion pay" in power, money or status. Rather, it was those who were predisposed to take risks who were drawn to him. He invited people to a totally new and uncharted kind of living. Some followed that call to adventure during his physical life on earth, while multitudes responded a short time after his death and resurrection. And millions upon millions have done so ever since. The Bible accounts for the remarkable difference in that response by pointing to the power of a new presence in the world: the Holy Spirit.

The Mysterious Presence

Jesus promised that the Spirit would come upon his disciples and that his presence among and within those who believed in him would be transforming. He promised them a new boldness, a new vision, a new confidence in the message he would give them to preach, a new ability to help others, a new moral authority, and a new peace in the midst of turbulence and opposition.[13]

The record of these promises actually coming true makes the book of Acts exciting reading. Not only was their speech bold and effective, and not only did they show great courage and calm in the face of official opposition, but they created a fellowship within which people found freedom from a possessiveness about property, a divisiveness about distinctions of class and race, and a deceitfulness about matters personal and private.[14]

It was to the Spirit of Jesus, the Holy Spirit, that the apostles credited whatever changes in personal behavior they manifested and whatever unity they achieved. He was the one who took the truths which Jesus had taught and which St. Paul had elaborated on and made them work in their experience. It is a matter of public record that these men and women had a message of hope in the face of death and of courage in the face of suffering. They were driven by an intensity of purpose that even the might of Rome could not withstand, and they looked on their day-to-day experiences (even the not infrequent stays in prison) as joyous adventures. They were pragmatists in the areas which count.[15]

Until recently modern psychiatric thought would have branded these early religious enthusiasts as neurotic rather than early pragmatists! However, the mood has changed. Contemporary challenges to this tenacious stereotype are found even in the *Journal of Religion and Health*. Two psychiatrists quote Abraham Maslow as saying: "The great majority of conversions reported by presumably normal people may be and often are described completely within the scope of the characteristic terms of the peak-experience."[16]

An interesting study in *The American Journal of Psychiatry* traced the experience of a group of university students who had experienced what they called a religious conversion. Before their experience they were involved in the typical college scene: drugs, sex and the quest for meaningful relationships. But each confessed that they had been uniformly dissatisfied with themselves, that they felt an incapacity to give and receive love, and that they felt a gap between their personal morality and their social conscience. They also expressed a vague sense of restlessness and confusion over the meaning of their college experience and what they wanted to do with their lives.

Harvard psychiatrist Armand Nicholi reported that there were marked improvements in virtually all of these areas as a result of their

Christian experience. Coupled with substantial healing in these very areas of unfulfillment went a new excitement over their studies (though many had been good students before), a commitment to the so-called helping professions (ministry, medicine, psychological counseling), a new respect for their bodies and a staunch belief in the importance of family relationships. The study concluded:

> These findings suggest that religious conversion may be one of the most profoundly transforming of human experiences, and therefore a phenomenon that psychiatry and psychoanalysis ought not to dismiss lightly.[17]

The Risk of Faith

During twenty-five years of direct involvement with the student world I became convinced that the basic problem standing in the way of wholehearted faith in Christ is not any lack of evidence that the records we have of the life, teaching and even miracles of Jesus are true. There is abundant evidence through the centuries, and even today, to the power of Christ to help those who experience the greatest needs: dying, suffering, setting goals and finding motivation.

The choice for or against Christ is often made more on the basis of what used to be called guts than it is on evidence. Will it be the country club, or a lifelong adventure that might mean social ostracism or even persecution? Will it be a six-figure income and a house in the suburbs, or will it be a life spent in service, perhaps in some developing country? How easy it is to sit with the agnostics and relativists, who are the conformists of today. How much more risky but adventurous it is to follow the one who said that to know him was to experience life in all its fullness.

In the seventeenth century most philosophers were rationalists and skeptics. One whom history hardly knows how to classify, because he anticipated some of the insights of later existentialism, is the French Christian Blaise Pascal. In addition to philosophy Pascal managed to excel as a mathematician (founding the modern theory of probability), a scientist (inventing the first digital calculator) and a theologian. In 1646, through an illness suffered by his father, he came into contact with the convent of Port-Royal and the intense spirituality there which was undergirded by a rediscovery of the grace of God through St. Augustine's writings. In time he experienced a dramatic conversion to Jesus Christ and from then on devoted his considerable energies to explaining the difference between a religion of rationality and one that was rooted in the heart as well.

As I mentioned at the conclusion of the previous chapter, Pascal is well known for his "wager"—originally his way of challenging the sportsmen of his day who stood aloof from serious consideration of real faith in God but could understand the language of risk. We must make a decision, he argued. We must stake our lives on the possibility that Christianity might be true. To choose and be wrong is to lose nothing. To choose and be right is to gain eternal life. Only if we wager on the possibility that the gospel is real do we put ourselves in a position to discover its reality for ourselves.

Curiously, the founder of modern pragmatism said much the same thing. Writing in 1848 Charles W. Peirce claimed that belief in God is more pragmatic than materialism because it offers more hope:

> In many questions of a religious and moral nature, a commitment of one's life to a position is required in order to test its validity. In these cases pragmatism will not only help to reveal the extension of hope and meaning that some of these views may provide, but it will also help to show our rights to beliefs of a positive religious and moral nature.[18]

This corroborates from the other side the fact that believers are more pragmatic than skeptics. It also supports the idea that one must wager on the possibility that God is real in order to discover that he really is.

I shall never forget my conversation with Emily at a rehearsal dinner before a large wedding in Boston some years ago. After getting over the embarrassment of discovering that she had been seated next to the minister at her friend's wedding, she talked to me on a wide range of subjects. When we got to religion, Emily was shocked to discover that I thought Jesus Christ more than a figment of history and believed that he was actually alive and well on Planet Earth!

She aired her many objections to the New Testament and to Jesus' personal claims to divinity, but was then stopped short when I gave a simple summary of our verbal progress to that point. "The point is this, Emily," I said. "If you are right, I am a fool . . . but what if *I* am right?" There was a stunned silence, and then she quickly changed the subject. A few weeks later I received an eight-page typed letter from Emily, detailing and defending her religious views and her continued objections to the faith. I had merely presented her with Pascal's wager in slightly modern dress.

The issue is truth. If we are to be more pragmatic than the pragmatist, we must remember that it is not we who judge the truth, but the truth that judges us.

Then the LORD said to Moses, "Go in to Pharaoh and say to him, 'Thus says the LORD, "Let my people go, that they may serve me. But if you refuse to let them go, behold, I will plague all your country with frogs; the Nile shall swarm with frogs which shall come up into your house, and into your bed-chamber and on your bed, and into the houses of your servants and of your people, and into your ovens and your kneading bowls; the frogs shall come up on you and on your people and on all your servants." ' " And the LORD said to Moses, "Say to Aaron, 'Stretch out your hand with your rod over the rivers, over the canals, and over the pools, and cause frogs to come upon the land of Egypt!' " So Aaron stretched out his hand over the waters of Egypt; and the frogs came up and covered the land of Egypt.

(EXODUS 8:1-6)

8

Frogs' Legs for Breakfast
The Hedonist's Bondage

AN OIL MAGNATE'S WILL STIPULATED THAT HE BE BURIED upright behind the steering wheel of his gold-plated Rolls Royce. In fulfillment of his wishes an immense hole was dug with the help of large earth-moving equipment. As the crane lowered the unusual coffin into the ground, a workman was overheard to say, "Man, that's really living."

Any philosophy has to stand the test of mortality. Has it got an answer to the problem of death? With no answer to this fundamental problem it is impossible to escape the nihilist's sigh that "all is absurdity." Conversely, it is also true that any philosophy must stand the test of life. Unless it offers a comprehensive answer to the major problems of living, it will either sink into oblivion or experience radical change in order to adapt to new challenges that living poses. Hedonism fits this latter pattern. As a system it has held appeal only to a very small minority of people, but its continuing influence in new and subtle forms is everywhere. Let me try to explain why.

Classical Hedonism

In its classical forms hedonism is the theory that pleasure is the only ultimate good and pain the only ultimate evil. One moral criterion alone is to be applied to any given action: Does it increase pleasure or does it increase pain? The word *hedonism,* from the Greek *hēdonē,* meaning "pleasure," together with the oft-heard Epicurean epigram "Let us eat, drink and be merry for tomorrow we die," are reminders that as a philosophy it has had cultured adherents as far back as the fourth century B.C. But if we take account of what Freud called the "pleasure principle" inherent in all desire, its origins as an approach to life could doubtless be traced back much further. From the Bible's perspective it is traceable to the primordial yearnings of man and woman in the Garden of Eden; Eve, contemplating the forbidden fruit, says, "It looks good; I want it; I shall enjoy it; I must have it; never mind the consequences for me or for others; consequences can look after themselves; here it is in front of me, and I am going to take it right now."[1]

Epicurus did not actually advocate the immediate satisfaction of all desire, but rather the maximization of pleasure over the entire span of one's life. It was the Greek philosopher Aristippus who taught that pleasure should be maximized now without regard for the future—in contemporary jargon, "Have a blast while you last." But whether long-term or short-term, hedonism reduces all moral questions into the simple equations: goodness = pleasure; evil = pain.

Over the centuries, and particularly since Augustine in the fifth century A.D., the tendency of Christian moralists to identify sensual passions with sin made theological orthodoxy a prime target of hedonistic attack. Because self-denial was at the center of Christian living, Christianity was perceived as inherently antipleasure. Bertrand Russell wrote: "The view that no saint would smoke is based in the last analysis upon the view that no saint would do anything solely because it gave him pleasure."[2]

Hedonists had only to point to Augustine's link of sexual desire with a fundamental distortion of our humanity to skewer the orthodox on their own rod. Although it is now realized that his views on sexuality arose more out of a reaction to the libertine lifestyle of his younger years than out of his study of Scripture, in this area he unfortunately influenced Christian thought for more than a millennium. Only comparatively recently have Christians realized that the "flesh" which St. Paul pitted against the "spirit" was not to be confused with normal physical desire, but rather it should be understood as that mindset which enthrones self while dethroning God.

The Sacredness of Sex?

Because of this unnecessary polarization of Christianity and sensual pleasure, attempts to set the record straight have had an appearance of self-justification. A. S. Neill, founder of a hedonistic, person-centered boarding school in England called Summerhill, wrote:

> Telling children that sex is sacred is simply a variant of the old story that sinners will go to hell. If you agree to call eating and drinking and laughing sacred, then I am with you, when you call sex sacred. We can call everything sacred; but if we only select sex, then we are cheating ourselves and misguiding our children. It is the child who is sacred.[3]

Recently a spate of books celebrating sexuality as a gift of God to be enjoyed to the full in its right context has helped to rescue Christian ethics and spirituality from unhealthy extremes. Commendable though this is, the tendency among contemporary Christian writers to eliminate false guilt has the danger of eradicating the concept of guilt entirely. Karl Menninger of the famed Menninger Clinic apparently thinks so. He entitled one of his books *What Ever Became of Sin?* It was the Western church's tendency to stress God's love at the expense of his justice and wrath that prompted Dietrich Bonhoeffer to write his flaming indictment of cheap grace in *The Cost of Discipleship.*

Today one hears relatively little about hedonism as such. Even the celebrated Playboy philosophy of soft-porn king Hugh Hefner is considered only mildly amusing—if considered at all. A Canadian news-paper quotes his last live-in bunny as insisting that he is finally now monogamous, as if readers actually cared. There are reasons for the disappearance of hedonism in its classic forms. For one, there is the frightening plague of AIDS and other STDs (sexually transmitted diseases). The media have pointed to a wide-sweeping reaction against the sexual revolution. Despite the "benefits" of latex barriers, it appears that the best guard against infection is abstinence or monogamous fidelity. The message seems to be getting through.

For another, there is hedonism's high susceptibility to linkage with various forms of human cruelty and control. Sadism justifies the infliction of pain on others by the pleasure it gives to the sadist. One can picture a sentimental Nazi hierarchy alternating between weeping over a Mozart concerto and joking over tours of duty in the torture chambers. This shows how pain and pleasure can easily be confused. Herbert Schlossberg points out that when feelings are elevated to the level of principle, viciousness is often dignified as moral. As Solzhenitsyn said: "Cruelty is invariably accompanied by sentimentality. It is the law of complementarities."[4]

The Politics of Hedonism

Probably the most searing critique of hedonism in the past half-century is to be found in Aldous Huxley's _Brave New World._ Written in 1931, Huxley's nightmare of Western society portrayed a population saturated with drug-induced good feelings and plenty of free sex, entertainment and technological fixes to stave off any negative thoughts. Political and intellectual freedoms had vanished, but nobody minded much because they felt so good all of the time. Huxley's vision was of a society totally controlled by technicians through the use of artificially induced happiness.

With great insight, Huxley saw that the use of sensual pleasure to exercise political control necessitates the elimination of intellectual and aesthetic stimulation. On the disappearance of real art, he wrote:

That's the price we have to pay for stability. You've got to choose between happiness and what people used to call high art. We've sacrificed the high art. We have the feelies and the scent organ instead.

But they don't mean anything.

They mean themselves. They mean a lot of agreeable sensations to the audience.[5]

The wide response to this book illustrated how easily hedonism could serve totalitarianisms of the left. About the same time Nazism was showing how it could do the same for those of the right. Those on the political extremes may have called for belt-tightening asceticism, but the purity of ideology was always open to corruption. Stalin called for "guns before butter," but enjoyed his vacations on the Black Sea as much as any other Muscovite; and Hitler, while extolling "purity" and strength, indulged in sensuality along with the rest of the leadership of the Third Reich.

But it is not only political extremes which are prepared to exploit hedonism for their purposes. Securing the good life for all has become a major goal of moderate governments as well. In fact, hedonism is necessarily more compatible with mild political leanings than with rigorous orthodoxies of any kind. Lesslie Newbigin, a respected ecumenical leader, in a book entitled *The Other Side of 1984*, charges that the pursuit of happiness, which was the Enlightenment's dream, came in time to be considered a basic right of the individual. And like all rights it must be secured by the state![6]

The High Cost of Pleasure

The decadence of lives given over to chemical dependencies and sexual compulsions of various kinds makes it easy to see that the choice of a hedonistic lifestyle has its downside. As the Exodus quote at the beginning of this chapter shows, God's judgments often take the form of giving us too much of a good thing. But it is not just those caught in the trap of various addictions who are to blame. Consumers titillated by the tabloids and gossip columns telling of yet another Hollywood hunk stricken with AIDS, or news of one more major-league player facing drugs charges, unwittingly contribute to the wider problem.

It is this wider problem that astute observers of culture repeatedly point to: hedonism saps the moral and intellectual fiber of society. In 1934 J. D. Unwin's comprehensive study *Sex and Culture* argued the thesis that "any human society is free to choose either to display great energy or to enjoy sexual freedom; the evidence is that it cannot do both for more than one generation." Or as Pitirim Sorokin, for many years head of the department of sociology at Harvard, put it: "The regime that permits chronically excessive, illicit, and disorderly sex activities contributes to the decline of cultural creativity."[7]

After several more decades of moral decline and with Unwin's and Sorokon's writing to point to, *Time* essayist Lance Morrow said much the same thing:

The deepest American dilemma regarding excellence arises from the nation's very success. The United States has been an astonishing phenomenon—excellent among the nations of the world. But as the prophet Amos said, "Woe to those who are at ease in Zion." It is possible to have repose, or to have excellence, but only some decorative hereditary monarchies have managed to simulate both. Success has cost Americans something of their energetic desire. And those Americans not yet successful (the struggling, the underclass) are apt to aim at ease, not excellence: the confusion contaminates character and disables ambition."[8]

I came across yet another testimony to the inverse ratio of sensual indulgence and cultural creativity in Pulitzer Prize-winner Tennessee Williams. No one would accuse him of showing unfamiliarity with the extremes to which sensuality can go. But shortly before his death in 1983, after having achieved wealth and fame, he wrote:

One does not easily escape from the seduction of an effete way of life. . . . With conflict removed, man is a sword cutting daisies. It is not privation but luxury that is the real wolf at the door . . . and the fangs of that wolf are all the little vanities and conceits and laxities that success is heir to. . . . Security is a kind of death. It can come to you in a storm of royalty checks beside a kidney-shaped pool.[9]

Hedonism and narcissism are of course linked. Both are experience-based. Both pursue the irrational, interpret love as sex and then make ethics relative. What distinguishes the two philosophies is that while narcissism is hedonism in neurotic pursuit of the self, hedonism is the self set free from all neurotic pursuits except pleasure. But similarities outweigh differences. Loneliness and meaninglessness dog the steps of hedonist and narcissist alike. Because individual pleasure is put ahead of the welfare of others, both necessarily lead to isolation. It is this inner isolation that, for all the talk of "freedom," is a terrifying bondage. As Bruce Lockerbie writes:

> In time, this essential selfishness must alienate every hedonist from his companions; and so, the carousel of pleasure-seeking, the endless round of party-going, must turn ever more inward, spiraling always towards total egocentricity. Spiritual and emotional vertigo is at last hedonism's only legacy.[10]

Hedonism's New Face

In the past several decades and greatly accelerated in the 1980s, there has been a transformation in the meaning of hedonism within American culture. Whereas the old hedonism was a revolt against the underlying values of the Western world, the newer variety is married to personal and national economic goals and fits in with the prevailing trends. These goals are no longer tempered by Christian values of service, generosity and compassion. It has been pointed out that the new breed of young urban professionals gives less to charities of all kinds and is less involved in causes than any other generation of Americans.[11]

America grew strong on a character-based ethic. Because you had to work hard with the land or with raw materials in order to prosper, the goal was achievement by honest perseverance in the face of tough challenges. But over the years there has been a shift from a character-based ethic to a personality-based ethic. In twentieth-century America and elsewhere, the route to success is achieved by working through other people, controlling their responses and manipulating them to your way of thinking. It is a management rather than a production ethic.

Success continues to remain the goal, but success is now related to other people's opinions of a person more than to what a person actually produces. With the gradual transformation of the United States from a production economy to a service economy, combined with the enormous power of TV to underscore the relative importance of public image over private character, the path to success has become increasingly divorced from real substance.

The old hedonism was considered an assault on the American way of life. Where embraced, it was as a conscious revolt against the deeply held character ethic of its day. What is striking about the new hedonism is that it dovetails quite well with the American way of life, where making a good impression is as valuable as making a good product.

The evolution of this change is traceable from the seventeenth-century Puritans who saw success as the blessing of God on hard work. For them material prosperity was not the goal, but the evidence of character forged on the anvil of hard work. Then in the eighteenth century the founding fathers of the nation had a new vision of success: the achievement of high ideals. Although many of these men were personally well-off, their goals centered on the quest for freedom in public and private life. By the nineteenth century still newer images of success were shaped by rugged frontiersmen for whom tough individualism became the ideal. Although Thoreau had his following, his vision of *harmony* with nature never shaped the national consciousness like Davy Crockett's *conquest* of nature.

Finally at the turn of the century a new kind of hero emerged: the robber baron. This was the gilded age of conspicuous consumption—mansions on Fifth Avenue and banquets with cigars rolled in $100 bills! William James criticized what he saw to be America's national pastime: putting a cash interpretation on the word *success*. Of course, his own theory of pragmatism was sorely tested by the obvious success of success, leading one to speculate that his protest was a case of "sour grapes"! But despite assaults on this materialistic view of success by the graduated income tax, the privations of the Depression and war years, the protests of the sixties, and the introspection of the seventies, it has predominated in America right up to the present. Today it reigns supreme and is the new hedonism.

The amazing thing is that all this has happened while America has remained the most religious nation in the developed world. With the highest percentage of regular attendance at religious services of any nation, the largest percentage of personal income donated to religious causes, the most frequent mention of religious phrases by national leaders, the burgeoning religious book-selling business, to say nothing of the widespread presence of religious broadcasting and telecasting, America outstrips any other nation in the outward tokens of religious commitment.

A 1981 investigation done by the Connecticut Mutual Life Insurance Company into the values of a wide cross section of Americans revealed that religion was the number-one influence on people's decision-making processes—higher than economic, racial, ethnic, sexual or educational factors.[12] Are we forced to conclude with Pitirim Sorokin that we have in America an increasing polarization of a sensate culture on the one hand with the extreme ascetics and mystics on the other? Or do we conclude with Alistair Cook who replied to Chesterton's comment that America is a nation with the soul of a church by saying that "it also has the soul of a whorehouse"?[13]

True Success

Clearly the strength of religion in American culture hasn't prevented the emergence of a new form of hedonism. But that probably owes more to a serious drift from biblical values within the broader culture—as well as, unfortunately, within the churches—than it does to some basic affinity between the American culture and the hedonistic vision.

If we are to evaluate a new vision of success, we must begin with the fundamental question: success in whose eyes? Until that question is answered we are still adrift in a sea of relativity.

I cannot measure true success in the eyes of my parents, however much I grow up wanting to please them. Freud and a host of others have confirmed the Bible's perspective that we cannot absolutize a parental value system, however much we may respect our parents as people. Nor can I measure success in the eyes of my peers—for which of my peers can assess my total family, professional and civic life? There are cases upon cases of great corporate successes who were tragic failures at home. One study revealed that half of those considered successful by their peers were unhappy people.[14]

This leaves me with one remaining absolute permitted by modern society: the self. Some will always ask, is it not sufficient to be a success in one's own eyes? But this begs a prior question of what standards we are to use in measuring our own success. Also, can we judge ourselves a success without affirmation from others in a society whose approval we value? Despite what we might say, even the most altruistic of us covet the approval of others. A former social worker confessed: "I realized that I would have to make a commitment to being poor to be a social worker. Eventually, I was able to shed the notion that to prove to everybody I was a good person I had to parade around as a good person by being a social worker." Thanks to a new career she and her lawyer husband are now able to manage on $100,000 a year![15]

In its own vivid language the Bible speaks of another set of eyes before which all success and failure is measured. "Everything lies naked and exposed to the eyes of the One with whom we have to reckon." "The LORD does not see as man sees; men judge by appearances but the LORD judges by the heart." "Your Father who sees what is done in secret will reward you." " For the Lord's eyes are turned towards the righteous, his ears are open to their prayers; but the Lord's face is set against wrong-doers."[16]

What these and other verses underscore is that there is only one final arbiter of right and wrong, of success and failure: God himself. He will judge, for there is none higher through whom judgment can come. But what of those who say that there are no values by which they can ultimately be judged? A world in which there is no judgment is of course a world where all values are rendered meaningless. Without a final word of some kind, we are left with a cosmic question mark.

Everything within us recoils from the absurdity of this conclusion. The continued insistence, even by many who deny God's existence, that there are some universals testifies to our innate conviction that right must ultimately be shown to be right and wrong wrong. Otherwise, concepts like justice, fairness, compassion, love, honor, responsibility and virtually any value we could name are reduced to cultural conditioning, and cultural conditioning is reduced to force, and force is reduced to biology. Then we are back where we started—with a valueless beginning to all of existence and a valueless end.

Of course, our desperate need for a final word does not thereby establish it. But the need does help open our long-closed ears to the inevitability of divine judgment. Liberal educators may have got us to scoff at early revivalist preachers who dangled sinners by thin threads over the pits of hell. But have we come up with a better "final solution"?

Every time we make a moral judgment on someone else—a racist in Alabama, a fundamentalist in Iran or a pederast in the south of France—we are assuming a moral order to the universe under which both we and they must stand. Without recognizing this assumed standard, we run a very high risk of self-righteousness. By denying the existence of a divine moral order we put ourselves in the happy position of forgiving our own sins and excoriating those of others which happen, for various reasons, to offend us. And happy us, when the things that offend us most are the farthest away, such as South Africa, for instance.

Jean-Paul Sartre once claimed that the origins of his atheism were traceable to an experience of being stared at in a café. He felt that the staring man turned him into an object and thereby dehumanized him. If God is omniscient, then his gaze upon us must inevitably do the same, he concluded. Unwilling to deny his humanness, he denied the existence of God. While the eyes of God may have turned Sartre into an atheist, they have caused many a humble soul to seek divine mercy as the only consistent antidote to divine justice. Omniscience is only terrifying to those who do not see that "behind a frowning providence, God hides a smiling face."

Hedonisms, both ancient and modern, fail to take account of the fact that we must each give a reckoning of how we live our lives to a just and merciful Creator. By taking a short view of life, they store up wrath for themselves on the day of wrath, and make pleasure a final captive of pain.[17]

A Shocking Future

Futurologists will continue to debate the alternatives between a world gone up in smoke from a nuclear catastrophe and a world left to freeze in an encroaching ice age. But believers confidently assert that "he shall come again to judge the living and the dead." The *parousia*, or Second Coming of Christ, has been a part of every Christian creed since the first Christians prayed *maranatha*, "Our Lord, come."[18]

Anticipation of this glorious event has sustained many a Christian in times of persecution and has caused many others to throw caution to the wind in heroic lives of service. But one of the primary values of the return of Christ to the life of faith is to guarantee that personal holiness and social righteousness will not have been in vain. As

2 Peter 3 argues, the coming "day of God" should inspire repentance and true godliness of life, not just because all that is unworthy of God will be destroyed, but also because in that day all that has been worthy of God will be fulfilled.[19]

Twenty-fifth Reunion Blues

To recognize Jesus Christ as the world's great hope and the individual's deepest consolation is simply to step in line with a vast company of men and women who insist that immediate gratifications are not half as interesting as long-term ones. I smile at the hedonist's "pleasure now" or "success now" because I realize that getting *there* is only part of the fun.

Returning to my twenty-fifth reunion at Yale, I watched as Mercedes-Benz's disgorged prosperous-looking members of the Class of 1958 and their wives at the gates of the Old Campus. The program announced that former classmates were preparing to tell the rest of us about the lessons they had learned climbing ladders to success. Wandering along familiar campus pathways that first evening of the reunion, two questions weighed heavily on my mind: "Had I been a success? . . . What was success?" The occasion, redolent with nostalgia, demanded such questions be asked and answers at least attempted. After all, what had one to show for all that expensive education after a quarter of a century?

I tried to be as honest with myself as I could be. I refused to take easy refuge in pat answers that, after all, I had started this and done that. While I was thus musing, suddenly I remembered that a friend who was rector of a nearby church had invited me to join him and a handful of parishioners for their customary 5:00 P.M. Evening Prayer. I hurried across campus to St. John's and took my place as the service opened, still very troubled by the questions I couldn't shake from my mind.

We came in time to a familiar part of the service, recorded in Luke 2, where the aged Simeon picks up the Christ child in the Temple and blesses God with the words: "Lord, now lettest thou thy servant depart in peace, according to thy word; for mine eyes have seen thy salvation." Listening to these words, I felt a quiet assurance settle in my soul. All the anticipation of wise old Simeon's many years found joyous fulfillment in one moment's realization that there in his arms was the long-awaited Messiah. Such was the sense of completeness that this knowledge gave him, he was now ready to "depart—or die— in peace."

In the quiet of that service I discovered what real success was. It came to me quietly, but very clearly, that the only thing worth calling success was coming to the knowledge of God and being able to behold him in the face of his Son. It seemed to me a knowledge so profound and yet so simple that it made even the smallest accomplishment of great importance when done in its light. Having, thus, the answer to my second question— what was success?—I had also the answer to my first.

The Freedom to Start Again

Ever since Julie Andrews immortalized the story of the Von Trapp family's escape from Nazi-controlled Austria in the early years of World War 2, Baroness Maria Von Trapp has been a symbol of a woman with courage to start again. Together with her family of young singers she and her husband began a new life touring the United States and eventually settling in Stowe, Vermont, where they opened and then operated for many years an extremely successful ski lodge.

A devout Catholic, with an open heart to all who confess Christ, Maria Von Trapp occasionally accepted speaking engagements as a means of raising funds for worthy causes. On one such occasion I happened to be seated next to her during a small dinner before her address. We chatted about Hollywood's reinterpretation of some of the key events portrayed in *The Sound of Music* and then fell to talking about more important things. In the course of our conversation I asked her what were some of the greatest lessons she had learned through her long and adventuresome life. She gave me a ready answer: "I've learned that there is nothing more important in life than to find the will of God and do it no matter what the cost."

Within three weeks of that conversation the beautiful Von Trapp Family Lodge burned to the ground! Along with many others I recall wondering, "What would they do?" Retire on the insurance? Not on your life. Within months the funding for a new and larger lodge was secured, and today it stands a testimony to courage, yes, but also to faith.

The obedience to God's will which Jesus exemplified and called for in all his disciples is the antithesis of the "Buy now, pay later" ethic of hedonists, whether ancient or modern. The future is both too wonderful and too terrible to be ignored in the decision making that must be done day to day. Because that future impinges on the present, obedience becomes a way of being set free from immediate demands in order to make decisions in the light of greater realities.

Today, in addition to a mushrooming illicit drug business, we are seeing new technologies vastly increase the potential to give instant pleasure. These have rendered traditional hedonism's outlets tame. For example, male rats have been taught to turn on electrodes implanted in the pleasure centers of the brain, and they will go on pressing the lever to the point of physical collapse in preference to eating and drinking, and even in preference to copulating with an available female rat in heat. What of people? In the future we only have to hook up the masses to electrodes in their brains to obtain instant euphoria at whatever intensity or duration may be desired.

In contrast to our insatiable demands for pleasure, whether of the raw sensual kind or the rarified sophisticated kind, there is a freedom gained from obedience to Christ which offers a real escape from self-absorption and which enables pleasure to serve as a by-product of something greater than itself. These demands are the jealous gods of the modern age. When our lives are given to Christ, there is a peace that reigns in place of the tension these gods create. As H. Richard

Niebuhr commented: "The faith of radical monotheism makes relative all those values which polytheism makes absolute, and so puts an end to the strife of the gods."[20]

Before the Eyes of Love

What Sartre never understood was that the eyes before whom all of us will be judged are the eyes of love—a terrifying love, to be sure, but love nonetheless. The Bible's view of the end of all things is that everything must be brought before the bar of love. It is there that romantic and sensual love must be purged of their self-serving elements and allied with the self-giving love of Christ.

What made the eighteenth-century Venetian libertine Giovanni Giacomo Casanova not just a loathsome, but a tragic failure was that, for all his romantic exploits, he was apparently incapable of love. Not one of the writers of his colorful era bothered so much as to mention him. We know of him only from his own memoirs. It has been suggested that he wrote those memoirs in an effort to stave off the inevitable conclusion that a life of loveless passion is a hopeless failure.[21]

Out of the blue I received a telephone call from an old friend who was rector of a vibrant Anglican parish on the West Coast of Canada. A young woman in his parish, engaged to a college professor at a New England university, had experienced a renewal of her Christian faith and now had questions about the rightness of their relationship. Would I see the man and talk to him? When Carl came to see me one early June morning, he had prepared his defense well. No, he wasn't a Christian. Yes, he had been living with Marjorie while they were both working on the West Coast, and he couldn't see why God should interfere with the sexual part of their relationship. No, he didn't understand her reaffirmation of faith in Christ or why that should be a barrier to their continuing relationship.

Carl, who had been married briefly and then divorced, had fallen very much in love with Marjorie, and she had returned that love in ways that seemed entirely natural to both of them until God re-entered the picture. Marjorie's rediscovery of faith meant that she now wanted any marriage that might come out of their relationship to be "in the Lord."

Carl made no bones about his thoroughgoing skepticism and his distance from things religious. Nevertheless, urged to appear in my study on threat of the dissolution of his relationship with Marjorie, he came, defensive but eager to hear what I might say. We talked for more than two hours, covering everything from sexuality to the integrity of the New Testament witness to Jesus Christ.

Interested enough to explore further, Carl left with a copy of Sheldon Vanauken's *A Severe Mercy* under his arm.[22] I had carefully chosen the book because I knew its true story of how, through tragedy, the author's wife and later Vanauken himself discovered God's love to be stronger than the strong love they had for each other. I was sure this would point Carl in the right direction.

Vanauken and his wife, Jean, whom he called Davy, began their relationship as happy pagans and gentle hedonists. They were planning to sail to the South Seas as lovers—until World War 2 interrupted their reverie and sent Sheldon to sea on the decks of a destroyer! Later, in Oxford, England, through C. S. Lewis and a circle of bright friends whom they discovered were Christians, the "shining barrier" they had put around their very human love crumbled as God invaded the privacy of the relationship they had prized above all else.

As I had predicted and prayed, the book worked its own strange power on Carl as he pondered the call to put his relationship with Marjorie squarely in Christ's hands. Later that summer I had a letter from him. Very simply he told how, reluctantly at first, lest his change appear to be simply an effort to win Marjorie, he had opened himself to God. "Somehow it became clear to me this summer that I had to try submission to Christ; I had to try acceptance. And the rewards were so immediate, in the sense of a joy inside me and a real peace between Marjorie and me that I feel I must continue. I didn't even really tell Marjorie until several weeks later. I guess I was afraid people would think me shallow and fickle—having been unsure one moment, and somehow converted the next. When Marjorie had her wisdom teeth removed, I read *A Severe Mercy* to her out loud, with tears streaming and sobbing voice—heart-breaking but wonderful."

The sexual dimension of their relationship was put "on hold" (not without some struggle) until the deeper aspects could be explored. They found that Carl's newfound faith brought with it a new joy in just being together. Without sex, we "actually felt closer, in some paradoxical way."

Carl closed his letter as I shall close this chapter: "I'm new at this since it forces me to figure out the rules of the game for myself; but I can surely use all the help I can get. I feel grateful that my obstinacy and pride are finally overcome. I may actually be on the way to discovering Love."[23]

"Thou wilt bring them in, and plant them on thy own mountain,
   the place, O LORD, which thou hast made for thy abode,
   the sanctuary, O LORD, which thy hands have established.
The LORD will reign for ever and ever."

For when the horses of Pharaoh with his chariots and his horsemen went into the sea, the LORD brought back the waters of the sea upon them; but the people of Israel walked on dry ground in the midst of the sea. Then Miriam, the prophetess, the sister of Aaron, took a timbrel in her hand; and all the women went out after her with timbrels and dancing. And Miriam sang to them:

   "Sing to the LORD, for he has triumphed gloriously;
   the horse and his rider he has thrown into the sea."

(EXODUS 15:17-21)

From the Other Side
The Christian's Certainty

N COMING TO MY CONCLUSION I AM QUITE AWARE THAT no self-respecting skeptic reading this book will be convinced of the truth of Christianity merely by seeing how isolated aspects of the Bible's message answer the charges of thinking unbelievers. That is, of course, not my point.

I have tried to show that in fact the charge goes in the other direction. New Age philosophy offers a pseudoscientific vision of the creation that must face the charge that its view of God is not as personal as the people who espouse it. It is the biblical view of creation that challenges humanists to come up with a basis for their high view of human beings. It is the purity of Christ's life coupled with the finality of his claims that calls relativists to give an account of why they are unwilling to see any absolute save their own relativism.

Narcissists fear the loss of self in the gospel's invitation to die with Christ and be reborn through faith, but must confess they have no alternative path of wholeness to replace it. Agnostics must keep on asserting the impossibility of knowing anything about God, despite abundant evidence for the resurrection of Jesus and the testimony of many who claim to have come to know God through him.

The ability of Christians to face the facts of death and suffering and to engage life with a sense of purpose and adventure through the Holy Spirit's power confronts the pragmatism of unbelief with the pragmatism of faith. Hedonists, caught in the bind of a materialistic vision of success, must consider why people of faith see success in such very different terms and why the ultimate judgment of love apparently sets people free to be go-givers rather than go-getters.

Each part of the biblical witness offers its own exit route from the iron furnaces which skepticism erects. From God to Creation to the Incarnation to the Cross, from the Resurrection to the sending of the Holy Spirit to the Judgment, different aspects of God's revelation in Christ hold out the promise of freedom to those who may be looking for a way out. Another way of seeing this is to recognize that each of the *isms* we have considered is in opposition to some dimension of the truth. Each tries to build a view of life by leaving out some crucial aspect of the truth as God has revealed it.

Because people do not think in neat categories, few today define themselves as modern monists or hedonists or narcissists. This does not mean that their world view is not shaped largely by one or more of these *isms*. Just as modern secularists approach Christianity with the total weight of doubt from all the sources we have touched on, so Christians must reply not with some isolated aspect of the biblical witness, but with that witness as a whole. Only when Christians take time to do this and present the gospel well will the gospel message appear to be the seamless robe it is. For the gospel is true not just in this or that part, but rather true in its completeness—so that all other truths must be tested by it.

Logical Alternatives: Pessimism or Utopia

Despite the apparent variety of *isms* that continue to be with us in one form or another, thinking persons must extend the logic of their thinking, either in the direction of ultimate despair or toward some kind of utopia. Bertrand Russell's despairing cry in his essay "A Free Man's Worship"[1] has been echoed with less literary flourish and flair by many others who stand with him in the humanistic tradition.

Kenneth Clark, whose monumental work *Civilization* surveyed the enormous accomplishments of civilizing man over the centuries— especially in the West—concluded:

> The trouble is that there is still no center. The moral and intellectual failure of Marxism has left us with no alternative to heroic materialism, and that isn't enough. One may be optimistic, but one can't exactly be joyful at the prospect before us.[2]

The optimism one finds in the early part of Clark's book reveals itself eventually as a thin veneer over an underlying pessimism.

The same gloomy view of the future is found in Robert Heilbroner's *An Inquiry into the Human Prospect.* Opening with the question "Is there hope for man?" he continues by saying:

> The civilizational malaise . . . reflects the inability of a civilization directed to material improvement—higher incomes, better diets, miracles of medicine, triumphs of applied physics and chemistry— to satisfy the human spirit. . . . The answer to whether we can conceive of the future other than as a continuation of the darkness, cruelty, and disorder of the past seems to me to be no; and to the question of whether worse impends, yes.[3]

At the other end of the spectrum are the utopians, who, despite all the evidence to the contrary, still believe that the perfect society is around the corner, or, as my young student friend told me, believe in "the infinite perfectibility of human nature."[4]

The one hundred and ninety signatories to the *Humanist Manifesto II* still believe in a utopia to come, after all vestiges of traditional religion have, of course, been neutralized. In addition to humanists there are the new mystics like Theodore Roszak who believe that everything will once again be ONE, after technocracy and rationality have been replaced by the mystic vision.

Half-Truths

To reject these alternatives to Christian belief is not to suggest that there is no truth in them. Quite the opposite. Error is always fabricated from a string of half-truths. As criticisms of Christian orthodoxy, they are often true in what they say is false, but at the very same time false in what they say is true.

Their criticisms of many of Christianity's most ardent defenders often hit home. But to point to an apparent falsehood in a system or to ridicule its adherents does not establish the truth of another system. H. L. Mencken, the Baltimore journalist who combined pungent criticism of American life with a lifelong hostility to organized religion, said quite rightly:

> The world always makes the assumption that the exposure of error is identical with the discovery of truth—that error and truth are simply opposites. They are nothing of the sort. What the world turns to, when it has been cured of one error, is usually simply another error, and may be worse than the first one.

One cannot help wondering if there are many who could attest to the truth of his words better than he! A ruthless iconoclast, his witty but vicious attacks on public leaders endeared him to the intelligentsia, but cost him credibility with the younger generation. One wonders in the end what he did believe. "The older I grow," he said, "the more I distrust the familiar doctrine that age brings wisdom."

To establish the truth of any system we need to evaluate not only what it says is wrong, but also what it says is right. Moreover, we need to examine that "right" in its total context, not just on the truth of this or that assertion. People who "accept Jesus" because of the lofty nature of his ethical teaching miss the point. He should be accepted (or rejected) on the basis of his total truthfulness—in other words, does he or does he not give a coherent and reliable view of reality?

Consider Distinctives

Where we start is important. Nowhere does the Bible argue for the existence of God. It is simply not considered worthy of debate. Those who deny God's existence are called fools; and those who affirm it are wise.[5]

The issue in question in the Bible is not God's existence but his nearness. On Mount Sinai Moses was to "go near" to God and hear what he was saying. "Thou art near, O LORD, and all thy commandments are true," said the psalmist. The faithful were to call upon the Lord "while he is near." Prophets asserted that the "day of the LORD" was near. God dwelt in the high and holy place; but also "with him who is of a humble heart." What was so shocking to the religious establishment of his day was not Jesus' proclamation of the kingdom, but his saying that the "kingdom of God is at hand."[6]

This has always been the real issue. What set Blaise Pascal apart from the seventeenth-century philosophers of his day was not his theism, but rather his Christ-centered faith in a personal God who is active in our daily lives. Had Jesus called God his Father in some mystical, highly personal way, he would have been no threat. But because he demonstrated that God was *here*, working through him to heal, forgive, restore, judge and redeem people, they went wild. Similarly Paul explained the reason for his opposition: Men and women are quite aware of the existence of God, but have a basic desire to keep him at arm's length. Hence they "suppress the truth" of his nearness,[7] substituting for the real God gods that are kept at a convenient distance. Such gods never heal the lame, give sight to the blind or forgive the guilty.

Christianity's First Cultural Despisers

Both the educated Jews and the cultured Greeks of the New Testament period found this claim that God was active in our midst deeply offensive. Why?

To the first-century Jew it was scandalous to suggest that the holy God, whose sacred name no one hardly dared mention for fear of blasphemy, had consented to "come down" to earth, allow himself to mingle with ordinary sinners like tax collectors and whores, and then become the object of violent hatred in order to deliver his people from their sins.

To the Greek it seemed ludicrous to imagine that a God (who was infinite) could agree to limit himself to just one particular manifestation, that of a simple carpenter from a forgotten corner of Galilee, and at just one point in history.

To the Jews the Incarnation was a compromise of God's *holiness*, because God came too close to sin; while to the Greeks the Incarnation was a compromise of God's *spirituality*, because God had taken upon himself the limitations and restrictions of human flesh.

Isn't this the problem of thinking people today? Few really doubt the existence of God. It isn't necessary. What they do assume, however, is God's irrelevance. Pushed deep into the recesses of people's private lives and tolerated as an expression of personal piety, God is allowed to "exist"; but God is not permitted to be near and active as today's Lord of history and today's savior of humankind.

Convincing the Intelligent Jew

Jesus claimed that people need a spiritual rebirth in order to experience the kingdom. Nicodemus, his Pharisaic visitor in John 3, balked because he believed that God could only work through the natural order. Despite Israel's amazing history he had lost touch with a God who could act by direct intervention into the lives of people and nations. Listening to Jesus, he was unable to envision this new birth as anything but some kind of a re-entry into one's mother's womb. Of course the idea was preposterous, and he rejected it out of hand.

What you need, Jesus said, is a radical transformation of your entire world view. You need to see that God is near, like the wind blowing through the trees. If only you would receive my testimony, you would understand.[8]

Nicodemus might represent all those who are prepared to give Jesus a prominent place in their world view, but who are not prepared to give him the pre-eminent place. Society is full of those who admire Jesus, giving him a place of honor and respect, but who refuse to bow the knee to him as Lord and God.

I recall a cultured Jewish woman who once took tennis lessons from me at a summer community. In my tennis clothes I hardly looked like a "man of the cloth"; but word circulated amongst my tennis students I really *was* a minister! The woman needed work on her serve. Endeavoring to get her to relax as she threw the ball in the air at the start of her swing, I told her to flex her left knee a bit when she tossed the ball. I had to repeat my instruction a few times because the message wasn't getting through. With a rude awakening I discovered her problem: With all the defensiveness of a person who is fed up with being preached at, she looked at me and exclaimed: "I don't get down on my knees for anybody!"

Persuading the Philosophic Gentiles
In Acts 17 we find Paul in Athens in approximately A.D. 55. He has been granted a hearing with the esteemed leaders of Greek intellectual life. He begins:

I perceive that in every way you are very religious. For as I passed along, and observed the objects of your worship, I found also an altar with this inscription, "To an unknown god." What therefore you worship as unknown, this I proclaim to you. The God who made the world and everything in it, being Lord of heaven and earth, does not live in shrines made by man, nor is he served by human hands, as though he needed anything, since he himself gives to all men life and breath and everything. And he made from one every nation of men to live on all the face of the earth, having determined allotted periods and the boundaries of their habitation, that they should seek God, in the hope that they might feel after him and find him. Yet he is not far from each one of us, for "In him we live and move and have our being"; as even some of your poets have said, "For we are indeed his offspring."[9]

Paul continues by weaving his way in and out of their literature, building bridges to his audience by quoting their scholars: Epicurus, who said God needs nothing from men; the Stoics, who maintained that God was the source of all life; Epimenides, who said, "In him we live and move and have our being"; and Aratus, a philosopher who asserted that "we are his offspring." These quotes supported Paul's claim that God is both personal and knowable. The conclusion Paul draws is that God "is not far from each one of us." His curious listeners are still all ears, because they have not realized the full implications of what this Jewish preacher is saying.

Paul has now merely built up to his main point. Having gotten them to listen, he gives it straight: "The times of ignorance God overlooked, but now he commands all men everywhere to repent, because he has fixed a day on which he will judge the world in righteousness by a man whom he has appointed, and of this he has given assurance to all men by raising him from the dead."[10] At this astounding claim the audience completely breaks up. Hecklers interrupt, and Paul can go no further. Luke, the writer of Acts, records that the day was not without its compensations. Some did believe.

In both Nicodemus's case and the Athenians' case the fundamental problem was the claim, first by Jesus and then by Paul, that God was doing something right now. This demanded a response: a spiritual rebirth, a repentance, a submission to the lordship of Christ. Such demands were immensely threatening to educated people then. They are now as well. They shatter the notion of a God who exists as the object of a human speculative quest. They focus the rays of the sun through a magnifying glass until it suddenly bursts into flame.

The Question of Authority

Religious claims always raise the question of authority. It is no wonder that Jesus' enemies were always asking him, "By what authority do you do these things?" His answers were suitably nontraditional. He never said "I have been certified by the Rabbinic School of X"; or "Rabbi

Y has given me his endorsement." Nor, for that matter, did Paul ever cite the fact that he studied under the great Gamaliel as certification for what he preached. His one reference to Gamaliel was to certify his Jewish credentials, not his apostolic message.

Jesus replied to questions about his authority by saying:

Even if I do bear witness to myself, my testimony is true, for I know whence I have come and whither I am going. . . . Even if I do judge, my judgment is true, for it is not I alone that judge, but I and he who sent me.

Do you say of him whom the Father consecrated and sent into the world, "You are blaspheming," because I said, "I am the Son of God"? If I am not doing the works of my Father, then do not believe me; but if I do them, even though you do not believe me, believe the works, that you may know and understand that the Father is in me and I am in the Father.

For I have not spoken on my own authority; the Father who sent me has himself given me commandment what to say and what to speak. . . . What I say, therefore, I say as the Father has bidden me.[11]

If because of a superficial knowledge of New Testament studies you are tempted to dismiss these passages because they are all from the Gospel of John, thought by some to be written rather late, and reflective more of the devotion of the early church than of the exact words of Jesus, then read Matthew 11:27 and Luke 10:22 for exactly the same kind of language in the Synoptic Gospels.

Consider the dilemma of Jesus' listeners. Before them was a relatively uneducated Galilean who was undeniably endowed with amazing healing powers. None of the existing religious groups endorsed him. In fact, they were united for the first time in years—in opposition to him! Yet in reply to their question about authority, he simply stated that they had to choose. There was his own witness, and there was the witness of the Father, as demonstrated by the mighty works he was able to do in the Father's name. That was all, and that was enough.

The significance of this for the subject of Christian certainty is, I hope, beginning to dawn on you. Jesus asked for a decision about himself on only one basis: the absolute coherence of what people saw him to be and to do with what they knew God to be like. Again and again Jesus asked people to decide whether what he said and did had the unmistakable mark of God on it. He gave no other guarantees. People had to decide about him on one basis alone: the inherent truth they observed in him and the correspondence between what they saw in him and what they knew of God.

Today's skeptics have a similar task. Once they have a fair and honest exposure to the New Testament witness (and we know of no other Jesus than the one portrayed there), they must either dismiss the Teacher from Nazareth as a fraud or fall down before him in adoration and praise.

Can We Be Sure?

It is quite natural that, faced with such limited alternatives, people would try to proceed down a number of other pathways in their quest for the truth. All, unfortunately, are dead ends.

Infallible reason. The well-known ontological, cosmological, teleological, and moral proofs of the existence of God[12] may be helpful in providing a reasonable backdrop for a position of faith; but the existence of a God is not the issue. Philosophers or scientists might point to the inevitability of there being a Prime Mover; but no one was ever moved by a Prime Mover! Even if these proofs could yield solid evidence for the fact of a God, they bring us no closer to establishing the kind of inner assurance we need if we are going to launch out on a personal journey in submission to the lordship of Jesus. Nor can evidence of "gaps" in the evolutionary process leave us enough room for a living God who calls us to accountability and invites us into relationship *now*.[13]

Similarly, people claiming to have come back to life after being dead for a short time, who assure us of a realm of light and life on the far side of death, can at best only speak of a vague supernatural realm. Despite the research of people like Raymond A. Moody and Elisabeth Kübler-Ross into experiences of the dying, Hans Küng concludes that any attempt to build a belief in life after death on such an insecure and unverifiable foundation is at best a false security instead of a serious certainty.[14] In any case a vague belief in "something beyond" is not what Jesus called the kingdom of God. So reason, even when coupled with hints of a realm beyond the reach of time and space, cannot bring certainty. Like logic, reason is a tool for discarding what is misleading and affirming what is clear. But as a final authority it is inadequate.

Infallible church. The church has a vital function as the keeper of the Scriptures. It celebrates the truth and is the guardian of the "faith once for all delivered to the saints." But the church's role is a subservient one. Because it draws its life from the Word of God, and must continually be reformed by the Word of God, it cannot certify the Word of God to the world. To do that it would have to be above the Word and have a higher authority than the Word it certified.

Within Roman Catholicism the idea of infallibility did not take final shape until July 18, 1870, when the First Vatican Council declared that the Pope speaking "from his throne" *(ex cathedra)* on matters of faith or morals is infallible. Even then it caused quite a controversy and continues to do so through the publication of various books questioning its validity even within Catholic thought.

August B. Hasler, a Roman Catholic priest and scholar, argues that the vote at Vatican I was "rigged" by Pius IX who was, in the eyes of many, of questionable sanity at the time. Hans Küng says that the infallibility of the church, as distinct from the infallibility of the Pope, was "universally taught" at the beginning of the nineteenth century. However, Küng defines infallibility in terms of the church's ability to hear revelation aright, and makes it clear that all dogma is under the Word of God.[15]

The doctrine of infallibility, argues Küng, is like Communists singing "The party is always right." It is one thing to say that the church can formulate true statements of the Faith—even binding statements. It is quite another to say that it is infallible. And it is still another to say that the *Pope*, as opposed to the church, is infallible.

Infallible experience. There are many who would hope that an experience of the supernatural would convince them without a doubt of the absolute truthfulness of the faith. A young man once told me that he had seen Christ in his room and could almost reach out and touch him. This settled all doubt for him. The piles of crutches at Lourdes and the shouts of television healers are sufficient testimony to many who claim with utter certainty to have experienced physical healings by the power of God.

Others long for a quieter experience—one that would give a warm feeling deep within—something they might define as a "peak experience" in which everything came together for them as true.

I recall once explaining to a young man who was coming out of the drug culture that he should not expect thunderbolts when he prayed a simple prayer of commitment to Christ. He seemed to understand. We sat in a little outdoor chapel overlooking a lake, read some Scripture, and then he prayed a prayer of commitment to Christ as genuine as I can ever remember. No sooner had he finished than a thunderclap was heard in the distance. "Thunder!" he exclaimed, with eyes wide as saucers.

While experiences of various kinds do happen to many and warm feelings often accompany genuine faith, we must not rest our faith on these or give them the power to guarantee the veracity of what we profess. "We walk by faith, and not by sight," said Paul.[16]

Infallible Scripture. Some would like to settle once and for all the question of the infallibility of Holy Scripture, and then base their faith on the sure foundation of revealed truth. They point to fulfilled prophecies (which abound in Scripture), archaeological confirmation of biblical data (and it *is* remarkable), internal consistency (and there is clearly a unity to be discovered in the Bible's diversity), eyewitness accounts of events recorded in the Bible (and there can be no higher court of appeal than this for historical accuracy). Does not all this point to the Bible's trustworthiness, which, when combined with its own internal testimony to its own divine origins, makes a compelling case? Indeed it does.

The trouble is that general trustworthiness is not the same as infallibility. Our belief in the infallibility of Scripture arises not from an ability to prove that Scripture is perfect from start to finish. Rather it rests on Jesus' own witness to Scripture. He believed and taught that it was the Word of God and therefore inherently trustworthy. Our belief in Scripture is dependent on our belief in Jesus.

How then can we use Scripture to prove Jesus when we first need Jesus to authenticate Scripture? To begin with an infallible Scripture is to put the cart before the horse.

Truth

The basis for Christian certainty does not lie in the presumed infallibility of any external authority.[17] Later, as a believer, one holds in deep respect each of these witnesses. Scripture first, then the church, experience and sanctified reason are all crucial in determining the full dimensions of revelation. But these cannot guarantee the truth of that revelation to us in the first place.

Our only certainty lies in the inherent truthfulness of truth itself. But bear in mind, when we think of truth as something purely intellectual, we are taking far too "Greek" an approach. Truth must present itself to the totality of our being: mind, spirit, will and body. That is why Jesus insisted that no one would ever finally know whether he was sent from God unless he was willing to obey him.[18] Obedience to Christ is the way we submit our wills to God, and it is only when we are willing to receive from God in humility that he can reveal to us the truth.

It has to work this way. God cannot be the object of our knowledge, as if we could sit "here" and contemplate him "there." On the contrary, God is the subject and we are the objects. He takes the initiative toward us, and always has. God is not primarily someone _we_ know, but someone who knows _us_. Another way of saying this is that the root certainty which the Christian has is not "I think." It is "I am thought"; not "I know," but "I am known." Ours is the certainty that we are deeply known by God, a certainty that, as P. T. Forsyth wrote, "shows as faith when we weave it into practical life."[19]

Emile Cailliet put this in a refreshing way when he described how he became a Christian. As a young French scholar in search of truth, he spent years studying the great philosophers and taking notes on their writings. After nearly a decade of this he read his notes and was profoundly disappointed. "I shall write my own philosophy," he said to himself and proceeded to do so. After another decade he reviewed his work. Again he was disappointed. He had that same empty feeling he got when he read the great philosophers.

Coming home one day he found his wife reading the Bible. "Get that book of superstition out of this house," he said. She refused and pleaded with him to give it at least a superficial glance. He agreed, reluctantly. But then he found that the more he read, the more engrossed he became in the text. In the end Cailliet became a convinced Christian and in time went on to spend many of his most creative years as a professor at Princeton Theological Seminary. His description of that fresh encounter with the Bible struck me as authentic. He wrote: "At last I found a book which understands me!"

Multitudes have had a similar experience. Turning to the Bible to study Jesus, they have discovered to their joy or their embarrassment that it is he who is in reality studying them.

The ultimate fact about the universe is a personal God. Therefore, truth comes to us in a highly personal way. We ask God for the truth, and he shows us his Son. Revelation is not God's gift of truth as much as it is the gift of God's own personal self.[20]

While Sartre feared God's gaze, we delight in it. The knowledge that the God of the universe sees and understands us totally, and, despite that knowledge, fully accepts us, brings a highly personal kind of certainty. It is not the certainty of facts, it is the certainty of knowing that we are loved.

Scripture has a vital role to play—but not as the donor of certainty. "Faith comes by hearing and hearing by the preaching of Christ," said Paul.[21] The Christian discovers that when Christ is preached in faithfulness to Scripture, then the Spirit takes the written Word and transforms it into a life-giving Word. We do not go to the Scriptures to find truth, we go to them to listen to God and to meet with him as we might read and reread a cherished letter from a friend. Holy Scripture is not the donor of certainty. It is the gift to us from a certain donor.[22]

The Missing Chapter

In addition to our being the subjects of God's total and loving knowledge, there is another basis on which we recognize the inherent truthfulness of truth. This is truth's comprehensiveness. Truth ties together the whole of reality. Imagine for a minute that you picked off your bookshelf at home an autobiography of a fairly recent ancestor. You begin to read it and become totally involved. But halfway through the book you discover that a crucial chapter is missing. The story is too interesting to put down, so you proceed to finish the book, doing your best to figure out what the missing chapter contains. When you reach the end, there are a hundred questions left hanging, of course. You wonder: do I have the story as it really is?

Years later you are cleaning out the attic, and at the bottom of a box of papers you find a section of a book that apparently had once fallen out of its binding. You glance at it, and to your delight it is the missing chapter of the autobiography you once read. Eagerly you find a lamp and a chair and proceed to read. "Yes, yes," you say. "It fits! I can see now how it all hangs together." When you finish the chapter you sit back and contemplate the story as a whole. Now you say it *all* makes sense.

Our certainty as Christians is of this order. Apart from Jesus Christ there are great gaps in our understanding of life. He presents himself as the missing chapter of our autobiography. He invites us to put him not at the periphery of life, but at its very center. Once done, we know him to be true, because he causes the whole story to make sense.

In our quest for meaning, if we start with purely materialist assumptions, we are at a great disadvantage. We struggle to lift humankind up in the evolutionary spiral to a level where purpose and value and goals can be affirmed. But how, on materialist assumptions, can these things be accounted for? Materialism simply cannot account for art, music, ethics, the sense of purpose, even the value of scientific endeavor itself. Why not? Because by logic materialism must reduce all these to some accidental configuration of atoms in a long chain of cause and effect. Christianity is true, as C. S. Lewis wrote, because it can account not only for itself but also for the rest of what we call reality.[23]

Taking the Step

Truth in the person of Jesus Christ, the only Son of God, needs a response. Because it commends itself to our minds and emotions and wills, it requires a response from the total person. In Christ, through the proclamation of the Word of God when enlivened by the Spirit, God himself draws near. That nearness forces choice. We have the choice of suppressing the truth that invades our lives and attempting to keep him at arm's length. Many choose that path. But we also have the choice of bowing before him in the joyful submission which the Bible calls repentance and faith. When we do, we begin the path of discipleship.

Christianity is not a position, it is a pilgrimage. As the earliest Christians, who were called people of "the way," discovered, certainty comes as we walk the way of Christ. We find it true as we take step after step because we sense that we are being accompanied by a truth-telling God.

If, having begun to walk the "way," we veer from it, we may lose the certainty of our faith. As Bonhoeffer insisted, "only those who believe, obey; and only those who obey, believe."[24] In other words, since God commands us to believe, the act of believing in God's Son is a step of obedience. But by the same token, there is only one thing that will sustain that faith—an ongoing life of obedience. Obedience and faith are thus inextricably intertwined, just as are truth and love. The Word of God, which calls us out of the iron furnace and took human flesh in Jesus Christ, makes a total claim on us: mind, emotions and will. It is only when we respond with our whole selves to all that God has spoken that we begin to discover in our own experience that the God of the Bible is a truth-telling God.

Notes

Chapter 1: I Have a Dream

[1]C. S. Lewis, *God in the Dock* (Grand Rapids: Eerdmans, 1970), p. 90.

[2]Lynn White, Jr., "The Historical Roots of Our Ecologic Crisis," *Science* 155 (March 1967):1203-7.

[3]1 Corinthians 12:3.

[4]Acts 2:47.

[5]J. W. C. Wand, *A History of the Early Church to A.D. 500* (London: Methuen & Co., 1937), pp. 37ff.

[6]1 Corinthians 15:17.

[7]Quoted in J. V. Langmead Casserley, *Apologetics and Evangelism* (Philadelphia: Westminster, 1962), p. 44.

[8]Ibid., p. 92.

[9]Archbishop Desmond Tutu: "The only way forward is to overthrow the government by force" *(Sunday Times,* London, January 26, 1986).

[10]*Hamlet,* act I, scene 3.

[11]Tryon Edwards, in *The New Dictionary of Thoughts,* quoted in *The International Dictionary of Thoughts,* ed. John P. Bradley, Leo F. Daniels, Thomas C. Jones (Chicago: J. D. Ferguson Publishing Company, 1969), p. 48.

[12]Kenneth Keniston, *The Uncommitted* (New York: Dell, 1960), p. 60.

[13]Quoted in *The International Dictionary of Thoughts,* p. 49.

[14]Vance Packard, *The Hidden Persuaders* (New York: Simon & Schuster, 1958), p. 139.

[15]Matthew 22:37, interpreting Deuteronomy 6:5.

[16]Said by the astronomer Laplace to Napoleon when the latter rebuked him for not bringing God into his theory of the heavenly bodies (Michael Green, *Runaway World* [Downers Grove, Ill.: InterVarsity Press, 1968], p. 40).

[17]Malcolm Muggeridge, *The End of Christendom* (Grand Rapids: Eerdmans, 1980), p. 17.

[18]1 Peter 3:15 (JBP).

[19]Harry Blamires, *The Christian Mind* (London: SPCK, 1963).

[20]Lewis, *God in the Dock*, p. 91.
[21]Ibid.
[22]Adam Smith, *Powers of Mind* (New York: Random House, 1976), reviewed by Eleanor Links Hoover in *Saturday Review*, March 20, 1976, p. 24.
[23]Anthony Campolo, *A Reasonable Doubt* (Waco: Word Books, 1983), p. 42.
[24]1 Corinthians 1:23.
[25]Kenneth L. Pike, *With Heart and Mind* (Grand Rapids: Eerdmans, 1962), p. 94.
[26]Richard Holloway, ed., *The Anglican Tradition* (Toronto: Anglican Book Centre, 1984), p. 13.
[27]Corinth's 2,000-foot granite mound, called the acrocorinth, was graced by a temple to Aphrodite, goddess of love. Normally some 1,000 prostitutes, priestesses of Aphrodite, plied their trade in the streets of the city during the night and retreated to their sanctuary on the heights during the day.
[28]Harvey Cox, *The Secular City* (New York: Macmillan, 1965); John A. T. Robinson, *Honest to God* (London: SCM Press, 1963).
[29]Peter L. Berger, *Rumor of Angels* (Garden City, N. J.: Doubleday, 1969), p. 61-94.
[30]Bernard Ramm, *Varieties of Christian Apologetics* (Grand Rapids: Baker, 1962), pp. 107-24.
[31]R. C. Sproul, *Classical Apologetics* (Grand Rapids: Zondervan, 1984), p. 287.

Chapter 2: Barefoot in the Sand
[1]Tom F. Driver and Robert Pack, eds., *Poems of Doubt and Belief* (New York: Macmillan, 1964), p. 205.
[2]Allan Bloom, *The Closing of the American Mind* (New York: Simon & Schuster, Inc., 1987), p. 27.
[3]Morris Berman, *The Reenchantment of the World* (Ithaca, N.Y.: Cornell University Press, 1982).
[4]*Religious Faith and Twentieth Century Man*, pp. 51-52, quoted in Colin Chapman, *The Case for Christianity* (Grand Rapids: Eerdmans, 1981), p. 201.
[5]From *The Upanishads*, trans. Juan Mascaró (Harmondsworth: Penguin, 1965), p. 117.
[6]For a helpful discussion of the differences between various types of monism and pantheism and Christian theism, see Robert Brow, *Religion: Origins and Ideals* (Chicago: InterVarsity Press, 1966), chapter 9, "Theism or Monism."
[7]E. Fuller Torrey, *The Roots of Reason, Ezra Pound and the Secret of St. Elizabeths* (New York: Harcourt Brace Jovanovich, 1984), p. 115.
[8]Torrey, *Roots of Reason*, p. 117.
[9]*Psychology Today*, October 1977.
[10]*Saturday Review*, January 22, 1975.
[11]Herman Hesse, *Siddhartha*, trans. Hilda Rosner (New York: New Directions

Publishing Corp., 1951), p. 116.

¹²*Saturday Review*, January 22, 1975.

¹³See Jeremy Bernstein, a professor of physics at Stevens Institute of Technology, reviewing *The Tao of Physics* in *American Scholar* 48 (Winter 1978).

¹⁴*Zygon* 19, no.2 (June 1984):254.

¹⁵*Christianity Today*, May 16, 1986, p. 19.

¹⁶Robinson, *Honest to God*, p. 130.

¹⁷William Braden, *The Private Sea, LSD and the Search for God* (Chicago: Quadrangle Books, 1967), explores the interrelationship of the drug movement and directions in modern theology, especially chapter 9, "The New Theology."

¹⁸*Theology*, January 1985.

¹⁹*Christianity Today*, March 23, 1979, p. 37.

²⁰*Aurora Leigh*, book 7, line 820.

²¹Numbers 12:3.

²²John 10:34-36.

Chapter 3: View From Pharaoh's Porch

¹H. J. Blackham, ed., *Objections to Humanism* (Philadelphia: J. B. Lippincott Company, 1963), p. 11.

²Alan Richardson, *The Bible in the Age of Science* (Philadelphia: Westminster, 1961), p. 15ff.

³*Humanist Manifesto II*, p. 13.

⁴Blackham, *Objections*, p. 11.

⁵Quoted in *Time Magazine*, November 7, 1977.

⁶"Using technology wisely, we can control our environment, conquer poverty, markedly reduce disease, extend our life-span, significantly modify our behavior, alter the course of human evolution and cultural development, unlock vast new powers, and provide humankind with unparalleled opportunity for achieving an abundant and meaningful life" *(Humanist Manifesto II*, p. 14).

⁷Os Guinness, *The Dust of Death* (Downers Grove, Ill.: InterVarsity Press, 1973), pp. 10-11.

⁸Herbert Schlossberg, *Idols for Destruction* (Nashville: Thomas Nelson, 1983), p. 80.

⁹Ibid.

¹⁰Ibid.

¹¹Ibid., chapter 2, "Idols of Humanity," pp. 39-87. "Humanism is a philosophy of death. It embraces death, wishes a good death, speaks of the horrible burdens of living for the baby who is less than perfect, for the sick person in pain. It is intolerable to live, cruel to be forced to live, but blessed to die. It is unfair to have to care for the helpless, and therefore merciful to kill. Those who wish to go on living, it seems, are guilty and ungrateful wretches dissipating the energies of the 'loved ones' who have better uses for the

estate than paying medical bills" (p. 82).

[12]*Humanist Manifesto II,* p. 23.

[13]Fawn Brodie, *Thomas Jefferson* (New York: Norton, 1974), p. 432.

[14]Blackham, *Objections,* p. 106.

[15]George Carey, *I Believe in Man* (Grand Rapids: Eerdmans, 1977), p. 34.

[16]*Humanist Manifesto II,* p. 17.

[17]Friedrich Nietzsche, *The Will to Power,* 1-2, quoted in Guinness, *Dust of Death,* p. 12.

[18]Reinhold Niebuhr, *The Nature and Destiny of Man* (New York: Charles Scribner's Sons, 1949), p. 3.

[19]Quoted in Carey, *I Believe in Man,* p. 31.

[20]James W. Sire, *The Universe Next Door* (Downers Grove, Ill.: InterVarsity Press, 1976), p. 93.

[21]See Carey, *I Believe in Man,* p. 13.

[22]Genesis 1:26.

[23]Genesis 1:26; 2:19.

[24]See, for instance, injunctions to leave the land fallow during the seventh year so that it can "rest" (Ex 23:10-11).

[25]Genesis 1:28, 29, 31; 2:18; 3:8.

Chapter 4: Having It Both Ways

[1]Matthew 27:11.

[2]Quoted in Sir Norman Anderson, *Christianity and World Religions* (Downers Grove, Ill.: InterVarsity Press, 1984), p. 18.

[3]And as late as the early nineteenth century in Spain. Joseph Bonaparte abolished it in 1808; but it was revived briefly between 1814 and 1820. See F. L. Cross, ed., *The Oxford Dictionary of the Christian Church* (London: Oxford University Press, 1958), p. 695.

[4]Colin Brown points out that because the only real motive for obeying the categorical imperative is that it makes life more pleasant for everybody, it is really only a disguised version of the hypothetical imperative. Either we must do something because a transcendent moral authority requires it (in which case it is an imperative) or because we and others will increase pleasure (in which case it can only be, at best, a suggestion)—*Philosophy and the Christian Faith* (Downers Grove, Ill.: InterVarsity Press, 1969), p. 101.

[5]For a full discussion of Kant's effect on a unified field of knowledge, read Bloom, *Closing of the American Mind,* pp. 299-302.

[6]Paul Johnson, *Modern Times* (New York: Harper & Row, 1983), p. 4.

[7]Ibid., p. 5.

[8]Quoted from Driver and Pack, *Poems,* p. 206.

[9]Johnson, *Modern Times,* p. 48.

[10]Ibid., p. 14.

[11]Peter Kreeft, *Between Heaven and Hell* (Downers Grove, Ill.: InterVarsity Press, 1982), p. 40.

[12]Samuel Butler, *The Way of All Flesh* (Harmondsworth, England: Penguin Books, Ltd., 1966), p. 304.

[13]Kathleen M. Gow, *Yes, Virginia, There Is Right and Wrong: A Values Education Survival Kit* (Toronto: J. Wiley and Sons, 1980). The title is taken from the famous editorial "Yes, Virginia, There is a Santa Claus" which appeared in the *New York Sun*, September 21, 1897.

[14]C. S. Lewis, *The Abolition of Man* (New York: Collier Books, 1962), p. 96.

[15]Anthony Campolo, *A Reasonable Faith* (Waco, Tex.: Word Books, 1983), p. 150.

[16]Quoted in *Parade*, August 6, 1978.

[17]Matthew 16:13-16.

[18]Mark 3:21.

[19]John 14:6.

[20]Zechariah 9:9; Psalm 22; Isaiah 53.

[21]Mark 1:22.

[22]Luke 8:47; John 4:29.

[23]Psalms 19:12; 24:3-5; 51:6; 139:1-6.

[24]Matthew 22:16.

[25]Quoted in Howard Butt, *Velvet Covered Brick: Christian Leadership in an Age of Rebellion* (New York: Harper & Row, 1973), p. 12.

[26]Mark 13:31.

[27]Mark 8:29.

[28]Malcolm Muggeridge, *Chronicles of Wasted Time* (New York: Morrow, 1973), vol. 1, p. 81.

Chapter 5: A Cry in the Night

[1]Category 301.81, *Diagnostic and Statistical Manual of Mental Disorders*, American Psychiatric Association, 1980.

[2]Paul C. Vitz, *Psychology as Religion: The Cult of Self-Worship* (Grand Rapids: Eerdmans, 1977), p. 101.

[3]Ibid., p. 62.

[4]John 15:5.

[5]Matthew 10:39; 20:26-28; Mark 9:35; Luke 14:26; John 12:24-25.

[6]Allan Bloom comments: In asking students what books really count for them, "there is always a girl who mentions Ayn Rand's *The Fountainhead*, a book . . . which with its sub-Nietzschean assertiveness excites somewhat eccentric youngsters to a new way of life" (*Closing of the American Mind*, p. 62).

[7]Abraham H. Maslow, *Motivation and Personality* (New York: Harper & Row, 1954), pp. 46, 149-202.

[8]Watchman Nee, *The Normal Christian Life* (Fort Washington, Penn.: Christian Literature Crusade, 1961), p. 154.

[9]Fyodor Dostoevsky, *The Brothers Karamazov* (Middlesex, England: Penguin Books, 1958), vol. 1, p. 301.

[10]Matthew 19:19; Ephesians 5:29.

[11]Dan Kiley, *The Peter Pan Syndrome* (New York: Dodd Mead & Company, 1983), p. 126.

[12]Vitz, *Psychology As Religion*, p. 101.

[13]Paul F. M. Zahl, *Who Will Deliver Us?* (New York: Seabury Press, 1983), p. 10.

[14]Jeremiah 17:9.

[15]Timothy Dudley-Smith, *Someone Who Beckons* (Downers Grove, Ill.: InterVarsity Press, 1978), p. 28.

[16]Torrey, *Roots of Reason,* pp. 113-14.

[17]J. S. Whale, *Victor and Victim* (Cambridge: Cambridge University Press, 1960), p. 30.

[18]Quoted from O. Hobart Mowrer in "Sin, the Lesser of Two Evils," *The American Psychologist* 15 (1960):301, in Vitz, *Psychology As Religion,* p. 141.

[19]Christopher Lasch, *The Culture of Narcissism* (New York: Warner Books, 1979), pp. 137-38.

[20]Matthew 10:39; 2 Corinthians 12:10; Galatians 2:20; 2 Corinthians 9:6; James 2:5; Luke 9:48; Matthew 19:30.

[21]David K. Clark, in an article in *The Journal of Psychology and Theology* 13, no.1 (1985), argues convincingly that Robert Schuller's understanding of God's love for us is a distortion of the biblical concept of agape. Whereas biblically God's love creates value in its object, Schuller's God loves because of the "infinite value of the human soul."

[22]Luke 15:1-32.

[23]1 Corinthians 1:23-25.

[24]Zahl, *Who Will Deliver Us?* p. 66.

[25]John R. W. Stott, *The Cross of Christ* (Downers Grove, Ill.: InterVarsity Press, 1986), pp. 133-63.

[26]Mark 10:45; 2 Corinthians 5:21; 1 Timothy 2:6.

[27]Isaiah 53:4.

[28]I am indebted to Dr. Dean Borgman, professor at Gordon-Conwell Theological Seminary, for this story.

[29]Dick Keyes, *Beyond Identity: Finding Your Self in the Image and Character of God* (Ann Arbor, Mich.: Servant Books, 1984), pp. 83-84.

Chapter 6: Catch a Snake by Its Tail

[1]Franklin Baumer, *Religion and the Rise of Scepticism* (New York: Harcourt, Brace & Co., 1960), p. 128.

[2]Samuel Butler, *The Way of All Flesh* (Middlesex, England: Penguin Books,

1966), p. 94.

³John Knowles, *Peace Breaks Out* (New York: Holt, Rinehart and Winston, 1981), p. 68.

⁴Baumer, *Religion*, p. 142.

⁵Karl Marx and Friedrich Engels, *Manifesto of the Communist Party* (Moscow: Foreign Languages Publishing House, 1959), p. 21, preface to the German edition of 1883 by F. Engels.

⁶Karl Marx, *The Class Struggles in France, 1848-50* (New York: International Publishers, n.d.), p. 85., quoted in Baumer, *Religion*, p. 143.

⁷Baumer, *Religion*, p. 14.

⁸Timothy L. Smith, *Revivalism and Social Reform in Mid-Nineteenth Century America* (New York: Abingdon, 1957), pp. 135-47.

⁹Richard F. Lovelace, *Dynamics of Spiritual Life* (Downers Grove, Ill: InterVarsity Press, 1979), p. 373.

¹⁰C. G. Jung, *Modern Man in Search of a Soul* (New York: Harcourt, Brace & World, Inc., 1933), p. 120.

¹¹Lewis, *God in the Dock*, pp. 66-67.

¹²The Great Soviet Encyclopedia for 1950-51 in talking about the Old and the New Testaments says: "In reality both Moses and Jesus were only mythical persons."

¹³John Murray, *Life and Letters of Charles Darwin* (1888), vol. 3, p. 313, quoted in Colin Chapman, *The Case for Christianity* (Grand Rapids: Eerdmans, 1981), p. 192.

¹⁴David Berlinski, *Black Mischief: The Mechanics of Modern Science* (New York: William Morrow and Company, Inc., 1986), p. 270.

¹⁵C. S. Lewis, in an address to the Socratic Club, 1944; see *Screwtape Proposes a Toast* (London: Fontana Books, 1965), p. 58.

¹⁶*The New Encyclopedia Britannica* (Chicago, 1975), *Macropaedia*, vol.1, p. 311.

¹⁷Bertrand Russell, *Why I Am Not a Christian* (New York: Simon and Schuster, Inc., 1962). For those wishing to look up the passage in question, see Luke 12:10 ("He who blasphemes against the Holy Spirit will not be forgiven"). This is usually understood to mean the wholesale, deliberate rejection of God's revelation of himself as holy and loving and not some particular sin of the flesh as Russell probably once supposed.

¹⁸Brown, *Philosophy*, p. 227.

¹⁹G. K. Chesterton, *Orthodoxy* (Garden City, N.Y.: Doubleday & Co., 1959), p. 150.

²⁰Hugh J. Schonfield, *The Passover Plot* (New York: Bantam Books, 1965). Schonfield's handling of the appearances of the risen Christ shows one of the main weaknesses of his argument. Building on the failure of the disciples to recognize him immediately, he argues that these appearances were those of the messenger to whom Jesus had given the task of urging his

disciples to meet him in Galilee. In their enthusiasm and gullibility they mistook him for Jesus. But he obviously doubts his own thesis, for he also suggests another hypothesis: Jesus' "spirit" spoke to the disciples through the messenger, who acted as a medium in the spiritualist sense (p. 173).

[21]B. F. Skinner, *Beyond Freedom and Dignity* (New York: Alfred K. Knopf, 1971); Jacques Monod, *Chance and Necessity* (New York: Knopf, 1971).

[22]Arthur Koestler, *The Ghost in the Machine* (London: Hutchinson & Co. Ltd., 1967).

[23]D. M. MacKay, ed., *Christianity in a Mechanistic Universe* (Downers Grove, Ill.: InterVarsity Press, 1965), pp. 64-66.

[24]Acts 2:24, 36; 3:15, 26; 4:2, 10, 33; 5:30; 10:40; 13:37; 17:31; 25:19. Note that Paul's encounter with the risen Christ on the road to Damascus is told three times in the book of Acts (chaps. 9, 22, 26), and he asserts its absolute necessity to a valid faith in 1 Corinthians 15:17.

[25]Michael Green, *Man Alive* (Downers Grove, Ill.: InterVarsity Press, 1967), p. 40. Reissued as *The Day Death Died* (Downers Grove, Ill.: InterVarsity Press, 1982).

[26]Mark may have ended at 16:8, but the appearances mentioned in 16:9-20 are corroborated by the other Gospel writers.

[27]Galatians 1:18-24.

[28]1 Corinthians 15:6.

[29]Blaise Pascal *Pensées*, tr. Martin Turnell (n.p.: Harvill Press, 1962), quoted in Brown, *Philosophy*, p. 59.

Chapter 7: When Your Back's to the Wall

[1]Richard Rorty, Kenan Professor of Humanities at the University of Virginia, has written on pragmatism and believes it is "the chief glory of our country's intellectual tradition." He and a group of younger scholars around him testify to the enduring value of pragmatism's basic premise: that it is in the vocabulary of practice rather than theory, of action rather than contemplation, that it is possible to say something useful about truth. See Richard Rorty, *Consequences of Pragmatism* (Minneapolis: University of Minnesota Press, 1982), p. 162.

[2]John K. Roth, *Freedom and the Moral Life: The Ethics of William James* (Philadelphia: Westminster, 1969), p. 95.

[3]Thankfully, Susan Atkins, still serving time in a California prison but now a committed Christian, thinks otherwise.

[4]Schlossberg, *Idols for Destruction*, p. 58.

[5]Persecution of Christians in the twentieth century should not be surprising when one considers that 2.2 billion people, or 50.6% of the world's population, live in countries which either deny full civil rights or are actively committed to the suppression or eradication of religion. Recent liberaliza-

tion policies in the Soviet Union and China have relieved the situation somewhat. See David B. Barrett, ed., *World Christian Encyclopedia* (Oxford: Oxford University Press, 1982), p. 5.

[6]John 16:33.

[7]John Steinbeck, *The Winter of Our Discontent* (New York: Viking Press, 1961), pp. 41-42.

[8]1 Peter 2:24.

[9]Alan Paton, *Ah, But Your Land Is Beautiful* (New York: Charles Scribner's Sons, 1982), pp. 66-67, spoken by Emmanuel Nene to Robert Mansfield.

[10]Sally Magnusson, *The Flying Scotsman* (New York: Quartet Books, 1981), p. 129.

[11]Paul Johnson, "The Lost Ideals of Youth," *New York Times Magazine,* March 25, 1984, p. 90.

[12]Matthew 6:2, 5, 16.

[13]John 16:8-14, 33; 20:22; Acts 1:8; 2 Timothy 1:7.

[14]Acts 4:32-34, 5:1-11.

[15]Acts 16:19-26; 2 Corinthians 1:3-7.

[16]Abraham Maslow, *Religious Values and Peak Experiences* (New York: Penguin, 1976 [1964]), appendix A, as quoted by Raymond J. Wooton and David F. Allen, "Dramatic Religious Conversions and Schizophrenic Decompensation," *Journal of Religion and Health* 22, no.3 (Fall 1983):217.

[17]Armand Nicholi, "A New Dimension of the Youth Culture," *The American Journal of Psychiatry* 131, no.4 (April 1974):400.

[18]C. Hartshorne and P. Weiss, eds., *The Collected Papers of Charles S. Peirce, Founder of Pragmatism (1878)* (Cambridge, Mass.: Harvard University Press, 1931-35), vol. 5, p. 402.

Chapter 8: Frogs' Legs for Breakfast

[1]J. I. Packer and Thomas Howard, *Christianity the True Humanism* (Waco, Tex.: Word Books, 1985), p. 27.

[2]Bertrand Russell, *The Conquest of Happiness* (New York: Liverlight Publishing Corp., 1958), p. 99.

[3]A. S. Neill, *Summerhill: A Radical Approach to Child Rearing* (New York: Hart Publishing Co., 1960), p. 222.

[4]Schlossberg, *Idols for Destruction,* pp. 46, 168, see especially n. 80: From Aleksandr I. Solzhenitsyn, *The Gulag Archipelago, 1918-1956: An Experiment in Literary Investigation,* trans. Thomas P. Whitney (New York: Harper & Row, 1973), vol. 1, p. 202.

[5]Aldous Huxley, *Brave New World and Brave New World Revisited* (New York: Harper and Row, 1965), pp. xx, xxi.

[6]Lesslie Newbigin, *The Other Side of 1984* (Geneva: World Council of Churches, 1984), pp. 13-15.

[7]A. Lunn and G. Lean, *The Cult of Softness* (London: Blandford Press, 1965), pp. 148-49.

[8]Lance Morrow, "Have We Abandoned Excellence?," *Time*, March 22, 1982, p. 89.

[9]Tennessee Williams, "The Catastrophe of Success," *Harper's Bazaar*, January 1984, p.132.

[10]D. Bruce Lockerbie, *The Cosmic Center* (Grand Rapids: Eerdmans, 1977), p. 56.

[11]Charles W. Colson, "A Call to Rescue the Yuppies," *Christianity Today*, May 17, 1985.

[12]*The Connecticut Mutual Report on American Values in the '80s: The Impact of Belief* (Hartford, Conn.: The Connecticut Mutual Life Insurance Company, 1981).

[13]Quoted in Schlossberg, *Idols for Destruction*, p. 268.

[14]Douglas La Bier, Senior Fellow at the Project on Technology, Work and Character, Washington, D.C., as reported in "Success, The Chase Is Back in Style Again," *U.S. News and World Report*, October 3, 1983.

[15]Colson, "A Call to Rescue the Yuppies."

[16]Hebrews 4:13; 1 Samuel 16:7; Matthew 6:4; 1 Peter 3:12 (NEB).

[17]Romans 2:5.

[18]1 Corinthians 16:22.

[19]2 Peter 3:9-13.

[20]Paul Ramsey, *Nine Modern Moralists* (Englewood Cliffs, N.J.: Prentice-Hall, 1962), p. 166.

[21]See P. Schwartzman, "Fellini's Unloveable Casanova," *New York Times Magazine*, February 6, 1977.

[22]Sheldon Vanauken, *A Severe Mercy* (San Francisco: Harper & Row, 1977).

[23]Carl and Marjorie were married two years later.

Chapter 9: From the Other Side

[1]Blackham, *Objections to Humanism*, p. 106.

[2]Kenneth Clark, *Civilization: A Personal View* (London: British Broadcasting Corporation and John Murray, 1969), p. 347.

[3]Robert L. Heilbroner, *An Inquiry into the Human Prospect* (New York: W. W. Norton, 1974), p. 22.

[4]See chapter 3, p. 64.

[5]Psalm 53:1; 111:10.

[6]Deuteronomy 5:27; Psalm 119:151; Isaiah 55:6; Obadiah 15; Zechariah 1:14; Isaiah 57:15; Mark 1:15.

[7]Romans 1:18.

[8]John 3:1-15.

[9]Acts 17:22-28 (RSV).

[10]Acts 17:30-31.

¹¹John 8:14-16; 10:36-38; 12:49-50.

¹²(1) *Ontological:* The argument that says that the idea of God presupposes the existence of God. (2) *Cosmological:* The argument that says that life could not have started from nonlife. (3) *Teleological:* The argument that nonpurposive agents do not develop purpose. (4) *Moral:* The argument that the human moral faculty could not have been put there by humans themselves.

¹³Henry M. Morris, a creationist, writes: "At best, therefore, the fossil record can suggest only that different kinds of organisms originated at different times in earth history but not that they evolved out of each other! . . . We find great gaps between all the basic kinds, and essentially the same gaps in the fossil record that exist in the modern world" (Henry M. Morris, *Evolution and the Modern Christian* [Philadelphia: Presbyterian and Reformed Publishing Co., 1967], p. 34).

¹⁴Hans Küng, *Eternal Life?* (Garden City, N.Y.: Image Books, 1985), p. 14.

¹⁵August B. Hasler, *Pius IX: Papal Infallibility and the First Vatican Council* (Anton Hiersemann); Hans Küng, "Infallible?" *The Encyclopedia of Theology: The Concise Sacramentum Mundi,* ed. Karl Rahner (New York: Seabury, 1975), pp. 713-17.

¹⁶2 Corinthians 5:7.

¹⁷Webster defines *infallible* as "incapable of erring, incapable of failing: certain." But as used here, and generally by Christians, it is to be distinguished from *inerrancy.* Inerrancy is the claim made by many that, based on the fact that Scripture has God as its ultimate author, it is incapable of erring—at least in its original manuscripts. Most Protestant confessions claim Scripture to be infallible. Inerrancy is a word used in more recent years by some to make the meaning of that word more precise. I prefer to stick with infallibility.

¹⁸John 7:17.

¹⁹P. T. Forsyth, *The Principle of Authority* (London: Independent Press, 1913), p. 101.

²⁰Forsyth, *Authority,* p. 155.

²¹Romans 10:17.

²²See John 5:39.

²³See Chapter 6, note 15.

²⁴Dietrich Bonhoeffer, *The Cost of Discipleship* (New York: Macmillan, 1959), p. 54.

Bibliography

Anderson, J. N. D. *Christianity and World Religions.* Downers Grove, Ill: Inter-Varsity Press, 1984.

Barrett, William. *Irrational Man.* Garden City, N.Y.: Doubleday, 1958.

Baumer, Franklin. *Religion and the Rise of Scepticism.* New York: Harcourt, Brace & Co., 1960.

Berger, Peter L. *A Rumor of Angels.* Garden City, N.Y.: Doubleday, 1969.

Berlinski, David. *Black Mischief: The Mechanics of Modern Science.* New York: William Morrow, 1986.

Blackham, H. J., ed. *Objections to Humanism.* Philadelphia: J. P. Lippincott, 1963.

Blamires, Harry. *The Christian Mind.* London: SPCK, 1963.

Bloom, Allan. *The Closing of the American Mind.* New York: Simon & Schuster, 1987.

Bonhoeffer, Deitrich. *The Cost of Discipleship.* New York: Macmillan, 1959.

Braden, William. *The Private Sea: LSD and the Search for God.* Chicago: Quadrangle Books, 1967.

Brodie, Fawn. *Thomas Jefferson.* New York: Norton, 1974.

Brow, Robert. *Religion, Origins and Ideals.* Chicago: InterVarsity Press, 1966.

Brown, Colin. *Philosophy and the Christian Faith.* Chicago: InterVarsity Press, 1969.

Butt, Howard. *The Velvet Covered Brick.* Waco, Tex.: Word, 1982.

Casserley, J. V. Langmead. *Apologetics and Evangelism.* Philadelphia: Westminster, 1962.

Carey, George. *I Believe in Man.* Grand Rapids: Eerdmans, 1977.

Chapman, Colin. *The Case for Christianity.* Grand Rapids: Eerdmans, 1981.

Chesterton, G. K. *Orthodoxy.* Garden City, N.Y.: Doubleday, 1959.

Clark, Kenneth. *Civilization: A Personal View.* London: British Broadcasting Corp. and John Murray, 1969.

Cook, David. *Blind Alley Beliefs: A Christian Critique.* Basingstoke: Pickering & Inglis, 1979.

Cross, F. L., ed. *The Oxford Dictionary of the Christian Church.* London: Oxford University Press, 1958.

Driver, T. F., and Pack, R., eds. *Poems of Doubt and Belief.* New York: Macmillan, 1964.

Dudley-Smith, Timothy. *Someone Who Beckons.* Downers Grove, Ill.: InterVarsity Press, 1978.

Forsyth, P. T. *The Principle of Authority.* London: Independent Press, 1913.

Gerstner, John H. *Reasons for Faith.* New York: Harper & Brothers, 1960.

Gordon, Ernest. *Me, Myself and Who?* Plainfield, N.J.: Logos, 1980.

Green, Michael. *Runaway World.* Downers Grove, Ill.: InterVarsity Press, 1968.

Griffith, Leonard. *Barriers to Christian Belief.* London: Hodder & Stoughton, 1961.

Guinness, Os. *The Dust of Death.* Downers Grove, Ill.: InterVarsity Press, 1973.

Hartshorne, C., and Weiss, P., eds. *The Collected Papers of Charles S. Peirce, Founder of Pragmatism.* Cambridge, Mass.: Harvard University Press, 1878.

Heilbroner, Robert. *Enquiry into the Human Condition.* New York: Norton, 1974.

Hesse, Herman. *Siddhartha.* Trans. by Hilda Rosner. New York: New Directions, 1951.

Huxley, Aldous. *Brave New World and Brave New World Revisited.* New York: Harper and Row, 1965.

Johnson, Paul. *Modern Times—The World from the Twenties to the Eighties.* New York: Harper and Row, 1985.

Jung, C. G. *Modern Man in Search of a Soul.* New York: Harcourt, Brace & World, 1933.

Keniston, Kenneth. *The Uncommitted, Alienated Youth in American Society.* New York: Harcourt Brace Jovanovich, 1960.

Keyes, Richard. *Beyond Identity: Finding Your Self in the Image and Character of God.* Ann Arbor: Servant Books, 1984.

Kiley, Dan. *The Peter Pan Syndrome.* New York: Dodd, Mead & Co., 1983.

Knowles, John. *Peace Breaks Out.* New York: Holt, Rinehart and Winston, 1981.

Kreeft, Peter. *The Best Things in Life.* Downers Grove, Ill.: InterVarsity Press, 1984.

_____. *Between Heaven and Hell.* Downers Grove, Ill.: InterVarsity Press, 1982.

Küng, Hans. *Eternal Life?* Garden City, N.Y.: Image Books, 1985.

Kurtz, Paul, ed. *Humanist Manifestos I and II.* Buffalo: Prometheus, 1973.

Lasch, Christopher. *The Culture of Narcissism.* New York: Warner Books, 1970.

Lewis, C. S. *The Abolition of Man.* New York: Collier, 1962.

_____. *God in the Dock.* Grand Rapids: Eerdmans, 1970.

_____. *Mere Christianity.* London: Collins, 1952.

Lockerbie, D. Bruce. *The Cosmic Center.* Grand Rapids: Eerdmans, 1977.

Lovelace, Richard F. *Dynamics of Spiritual Life.* Downers Grove, Ill.: InterVarsity Press, 1979.

Lunn, A., and Lean, G. *The Cult of Softness.* London: Blandford Press, 1965.

Mackay, Donald M., ed. *Christianity in a Mechanistic Universe.* Downers Grove, Ill.:InterVarsity Press, 1965.

Mackinnon, D. M.; Williams, H. A.; Vidler, A. R.; and Bezzant, J. S. *Objections to Christian Belief.* Philadelphia: J. B. Lippincott, 1964.

Magnusson, Sally. *The Flying Scotsman.* New York: Quartet Books, 1981.

Maslow, A. *Religions, Values, and Peak-Experiences.* New York: Penguin, 1976.

Mollegen, Albert T. *Christianity and Modern Man: The Crisis of Secularism.* Indianapolis: Dobbs Merrill, 1961.

Morison, Frank. *Who Moved the Stone?* London: Faber & Faber, Ltd., 1930.

Muggeridge, Malcolm. *Chronicles of Wasted Time.* Chronicle 1: "The Green Stick." New York: William Morrow, 1973.

Muggeridge, Malcolm. *The End of Christendom.* Grand Rapids: Eerdmans, 1980.

Newbigin, Lesslie. *The Other Side of 1984.* Geneva: World Council of Churches, 1984.

Nicholi, Armand. "A New Dimension of the Youth Culture." *The American Journal of Psychiatry* 131 (April 1974):396-401.

Packer, J. I. *God Has Spoken.* Downers Grove, Ill.: InterVarsity Press, 1979.

_____. *Knowing Man.* Westchester, Ill.: Cornerstone, 1979.

Packer, J. I., and Howard, T. *Christianity the True Humanism.* Waco, Tex.: Word, 1985.

Pike, Kenneth L. *With Heart and Mind.* Grand Rapids: Eerdmans, 1962.

Pinnock, Clark H. *Reason Enough: A Case for the Christian Faith.* Downers Grove, Ill.: InterVarsity Press, 1980.

_____. *The Scripture Principle.* San Francisco: Harper and Row, 1984.

Rahner, Karl. *The Concise Sacramentum Mundi.* New York: Seabury, 1975.

Ramsey, Paul. *Nine Modern Moralists.* Englewood Cliffs, N.J.: Prentice-Hall, 1962.

Ramm, Bernard. *Varieties of Christian Apologetics.* Grand Rapids: Baker, 1962.

Richardson, Alan. *The Bible in the Age of Science.* London: SCM Press, 1961.

Rorty, Richard. *Consequences of Pragmatism.* Minneapolis: University of Minnesota Press, 1982.

Roszak, Theodore. *Making of a Counter Culture.* Ithaca, N.Y.: Cornell University Press, 1982.

Roth, John K. *Freedom and the Moral Life—The Ethics of William James.* Philadelphia: Westminster, 1969.

Russell, Bertrand. *The Conquest of Happiness.* New York: Liverlight, 1958.

_____. *Why I Am Not a Christian.* New York: Simon & Schuster, 1962.

Schaeffer, Francis A. *Escape from Reason.* Downers Grove, Ill.: InterVarsity Press, 1968.

Schlossberg, Herbert. *Idols For Destruction.* Nashville: Thomas Nelson, 1983.

Schonfield, Hugh. *Passover Plot.* New York: Bantam, 1969.

Shideler, Mary McDermott. *A Creed for a Christian Skeptic.* Grand Rapids: Eerd-mans, 1968.

Simpson, P. Carnegie. *The Fact of Christ.* London: James Clarke, 1952.

Sire, James W. *The Universe Next Door.* 2nd ed. Downers Grove, Ill.: InterVarsity Press. 1988.

Smith, Timothy L. *Revivalism and Social Reform in Mid-Nineteenth Century America.* New York: Abingdon, 1957.

Sproul, R. C. *A Reasonable Faith.* Waco, Tex.: Word, 1983.

Sproul, R. C.; Gerstner, John; and Lindsley, Arthur. *Classical Apologetics.* Grand Rapids: Zondervan, 1984.

Stevenson, Kenneth, and Habermas, Gary. *Verdict on the Shroud.* Ann Arbor: Servant, 1981.

Stott, John R. W. *Basic Christianity.* Downers Grove, Ill.: InterVarsity Press, 1958.

_____. *The Cross of Christ.* Downers Grove, Ill.: InterVarsity Press, 1986.

Torrey, E. Fuller. *The Roots of Reason: Ezra Pound and the Secret of St. Elizabeths.* New York: Harcourt Brace Jovanovich, 1984.

Vanauken, Sheldon. *A Severe Mercy.* San Francisco: Harper & Row, 1977.

Vitz, Paul. *Psychology as Religion: The Cult of Self-Worship.* Grand Rapids: Eerd-mans, 1977.

Whale, J. S. *Victor and Victim.* Cambridge: Cambridge University Press, 1960.

Zahl, Paul. *Who Will Deliver Us?* New York: Seabury Press, 1983.